O Little One

GIOVANNI PASCOLI

O Little One and Selected Poems

Translated by John Martone

Laertes

Chapel Hill, North Carolina

PUBLISHER CATALOGING-IN-PUBLICATION DATA

Names: Pascoli, Giovanni, 1855-1912 – author. | Martone, John, 1952 – translator, author of introduction.

Title: Giovanni Pascoli : o little one and selected poems / translated by John Martone.

Other titles: Works. Selections. English.

Description: Chapel Hill, North Carolina : Laertes Press, 2019.

Identifiers: LCCN 2019946514 | ISBN 9781942281054 (softcover : alk. paper)

Classification: LCC PQ4835.A3 A2 2019 | DDC 851.8

Laertes

www.laertesbooks.org

In memory of my parents
Mildred C. and John I. Martone
and my sister Diane

CONTENTS

xi

I. INTRODUCTION

Pascoli stands in the doorway. Born in 1855 in San Mauro (now San Mauro-Pascoli in his honor) near the Adriatic coast, an orphan (ten years old when his father was murdered, fourteen when his mother died of meningitis); never forsaking his attachment to the childhood nest and attachment to his sister Maria; a visionary of the past, who sometimes wrote the first drafts of his Italian poems in Latin (and many others in Latin alone) and translated Homer. He even limped like Oedipus, due to a birth defect of his right little toe; and like John Clare or St. Francis, he was drawn into the spell of little creatures. By the time of his death in 1912, modern Italy had been born, Ezra Pound had published his *Personae*, and Tommaso Marinetti had written his Futurist manifesto. The doorway looked out on a very different world.

Perhaps he hesitates—either too early or too late, a post-Romantic, "Decadent," proto-modern, the perfectly liminal figure on the boundary between daily life and myth. In *Beyond the Family Romance: The Legend of Pascoli*, Maria Truglio illuminates that elegant threshold to us, discussing the poet's work in relation to the Freudian uncanniness of everyday life, the nineteenth-century "Disheveled" movement in Italian writing, and Edmondo De Amicis's classic boy's book *Cuore (Heart)*.[1] Although Pascoli seems to have read neither Freud nor Jung, his poetics of the *fanciullino* (literally "little boy" but translated here as "little one") is rooted in a collective unconscious, a primal relation to the natural world, an innocence not so much lost as repressed over time, still transformative, if not wholly recuperable.

---

1. Maria Truglio, *Beyond the Family Romance: The Legend of Pascoli* (Toronto: University of Toronto Press, 2007).

1

There are many antecedents — in addition to those mentioned above, among the most pertinent, Giambattista Vico's association of childhood with the source of the poetic imagination in his *Nuova Scienza*. Consider two of his axioms (50 and 52):

> *Children possess a very vigorous memory, and thus have an excessively vivid imagination: for imagination is simply expanded or compounded memory.*
>
> *This axiom is the principle of the vividness of the poetic images which the world must have formed in its early childhood.*

> • • •

> *Children excel in imitation, and we see that they generally play by copying whatever they are capable of understanding.*
>
> *This axiom shows that the world in its childhood was made up of poetic nations, for poetry is simply imitation.*
>
> *This axiom gives us another principle. All the arts serving human need, advantage, comfort, and to a great extent, even pleasure were invented in the poetic centuries, before philosophers appeared. For the arts are simply imitations of nature and are, in a certain sense, concrete poetry.*[2]

Rousseau, of course, is another forebear, and in English we have Traherne, Blake, and Wordsworth — but Pascoli was prescient of an emerging evolutionary psychology. In this regard, two works from his library stand out in particular — a French translation of James Sully's *Children's Ways* and Ernst Haeckel's *History of Creation*. The former is notable for its attention to the development of language and sense of the child as an Ur-poet. Haeckel's evolutionary biology, visually gorgeous in presentation, clearly influenced the poet. Referencing the biologist in his preparatory notes to the *Fanciullino*, Pascoli observes that each of us carries within us the childhood of humanity, but Pascoli takes the scientist's notion in radically

---

2. Giambattista Vico, *New Science*, trans. David Marsh (London: Penguin Random House, 2013), 94.

personal terms, thereby anticipating modern depth psychology and the "inner child" of more recent psychotherapy. The *fanciullino* embodies the mythological *puer* of C. G. Jung:

> [T]he archetype of the child [...] expresses man's wholeness. The "child" is all that is abandoned and exposed and at the same time divinely powerful; the insignificant, dubious beginning, and the triumphal end. The "eternal child" in man is an indescribable experience, an incongruity, a handicap, and a divine prerogative; an imponderable that determines the ultimate worth or worthlessness of a personality.[3]

Pascoli stands in the doorway of revolution. Briefly imprisoned for his socialism, he ultimately comes to see the true revolution as interior. Thus he writes to his sister, *Andiamo dunque a fare opera. . . indovina, di che? . . . di emancipazione* (We have to create works . . . do you know of what kind? . . . of emancipation), a sentiment echoed in section VIII of his *Fanciullino*, and elsewhere. In retrospect it seems fitting that the young Pascoli's first teaching assignment was in Matera—a southern Italian landscape of mythic desperation (see Carlo Levi's *Christ Stopped at Eboli*) with its rings of cave dwellings that some see as a source for the architecture of Dante's *Inferno*. It was the home of Italy's great literary historian Roberto De Sanctis. At the time, Pascoli felt he had been sent to Africa (Italy's problematic *other* from the time of the Punic wars, to Virgil's *Aeneid*, down to Pascoli's time with Verdi's *Aida*, and beyond). He later dedicated a volume of his work to his students there.

Naturally, a nostalgia for a transcendent home goes hand in hand with Pascoli's poems of exile. For him the arch-poet of exile and foundation is Virgil, for example, but his antecedent is not the voice of far-ranging Roman imperium, so much as a poet of restrained and settled liberty. Pascoli takes pains to note that the word "slave" never appears in Virgil's

---

3. C. G. Jung, *Archetypes of the Collective Unconscious*, trans. R. F. C. Hull (Princeton: Princeton University Press, 1969), 300.

work. In their modesty and restraint, Pascoli would have us see Virgil and his contemporary Horace as the first eco-poets, ancestors of Gino Girolomoni, America's Wendell Berry and Gary Snyder, or Scotland's Carbeth hutters such as the poet Gerry Loose, who forgo the wealth of large estates for "a little field, not too big, with a garden, a fountain, and also a little woods." This is a life lived in moral harmony, the *fanciullino's* dimensions fitting "the instinctive wholeness of primeval times."[4]

In Italy, Pascoli is known for his love of the nest (*nido* or *nidietto*). Here, too, we see the archetype. He writes to his sister:

> [. . .S]*i chiede a che servono le mosche. Chiaro, che a nutrir le rondini. E le rondini? Chiaro, che a insegnare agli uomini (perciò si mettono sopra le loro finestre) ante cose: l'amore della famiglia e del nidietto. La prima capanna che uomo costruì, di terra seccata al sole, alla sua donna, gli insegnò una coppia di rondini a rondini a costruirla. Ciò fu al tempo dei nomadi. Le rondini viaggiatrici insegnarono all'uomo di fermarsi. E gli dettero il modellino della casa. Solo, l'uomo lo capovolse.*

> One asks what purpose flies have — clearly, to feed the swallows. And the swallows? Clearly, to teach people (thus they come to their windows) such things as love of family and of the nest. The first hut man made for his woman on the sun-parched earth, was a copy of what swallows build for swallows. Those were nomadic times. Migratory swallows taught people how to dwell. And they gave people a little model for the house. Only, man turned it upside down.[5]

---

4. Ibid., 390.

5. Giovanni Pascoli, *Primi poemetti* (Bologna: Ditta Nicola Zanichelli, 1907), ix-x. My translation.

We "turned it upside down," making the nest a roofed hut, but we also ruined things, forsaking the smallholder farm out of ambition for the large estate, turning from poetry-as-life—as Cid Corman put it—to self-serving theatrics (see section xvi below), of which of which Pascoli found plenty in his own day. Of this, more in a bit, but for now note how our impulse to turn things upside down informs the poetry of daily life:

LA QUERCIA CADUTA

Dov'era l'ombra, or sé la quercia spande
morta, né più coi turbini tenzona.
La gente dice: Or vedo: era pur grande!
Pendono qua e là dalla corona
i nidietti della primavera.
Dice la gente: Or vedo: era pur buona!
Ognuno loda, ognuno taglia. A sera
ognuno col suo grave fascio va.
Nell'aria, un planto . . . d'una capinera
che cerca il nido che non troverà.

THE FALLEN OAK

Fallen into its shadow, the dead oak
no longer struggles with whirlwinds,
and everyone says — Now I see: it was a big one!
Here and there last spring's nests
hang from the crown.
And people say: Now I see: it was a good one!
Everyone praises, everyone cuts. By evening
each departs with a heavy burden.
And somewhere a blackcap cries
searching for a nest it won't find.

5

The poem's restrained, objective focus suggests an affinity to his contemporary Rilke's *Neue Gedichte, New Poems* (published in 1907), whose *Archaic Torso of Apollo* offers a series of contrasts that tell us much about our poet.[6] Here we have a ruined tree in place of Rilke's time-ravaged sculpture, the pursuit of common light in place of a gas-lit candelabrum, and whereas Rilke's poem straightforwardly commands that we change our lives, Pascoli's leaves us with troubling uncertainties. If they could understand the warbler's plaintive cry for the missing nest, those peasants securing their firewood with so much chatter would be in any case oblivious to it, and their relation to the natural world is problematic. Once again, we stand uncomfortably on a threshold.

Pascoli's dilemma is part and parcel of his poetics. "The art of the poet is always a renunciation," he tells us, monastic and post-modern at once: creation is also erasure. This is nowhere clearer than in his discussion of ambition and the craving for celebrity. This *desire to be seen* rather than to *see* (or with even greater self-effacement, to *hear*) is the greatest threat to the imagination. The assertive youth can't understand the child. One suspects that Pascoli

---

6. My translation of Rilke's poem:

> We did not know his unheard-of head,
> wherein the eye-apples ripened. But
> his torso still glows like a candelabrum,
> in which his look, only turned low,
>
> holds itself and shines. Otherwise the prow
> of his breast wouldn't dazzle you,
> the soft turn of the hips breaks into a smile
> at the middle, with its fruiting.
>
> Otherwise this stone stood displaced and short
> under the shoulders' limpid collapse
> and would not flicker so like a predator's skin;
>
> and not break out of all its edges
> like a star: for there is no place
> that doesn't see you. You must change your life.

structures many of his poems as dialogues, not just as a way of paying homage to a tradition—the eclogues of Virgil and Sannazaro—but also because the dialogic structure removes the lyrical *I* with its self-importance. The double is pervasive in Pascoli's work. (He is constantly trying to break down or through binaries.) *Il fanciullino* itself has a dialogic structure, in which the poet addresses the deepest part of himself. For Pascoli, the poet aspires to an anonymity in which his poem becomes an object of nature.

Dante may be the father of the Italian language, but Italian as a national language is of more recent provenance, typically given as 1827, with the publication of Manzoni's *I promessi sposi* (*The Betrothed*), a frequent context for Pascoli's poems. To this day, Italy remains a land of regional dialects—often mutually unintelligible—as readers of Elsa Ferrante's novels will know, whose characters negotiate between Neapolitan and Italian. Americans who have seen Saviano's *Gomorrah* may find it a consolation that the original film contains Italian subtitles for the Neapolitan dialogue, but Luigi Bonaffini's anthology *Dialect Poetry of Southern Italy*, and blogs such *Poesia e dialetti* reveal the desperate vitality of such local speech—to the degree of *endophasia*, as P. V. Mongaldo terms it (an interior, private language)—in an age of mass-culture.[7]

For Pascoli, the languages of a newly unified Italy are only part of the mix. The poet was by training and profession a classicist. Many of his poems have Latin versions, and the contemporary reader may find it hard to understand, if not inconceivable, that for our poet, "La lingua dei poeti è sempre una lingua morta"—the language of poetry is always a dead language. Pascoli's essay, with which this volume concludes, offers a prescient understanding of linguistic change, the entropy which doomed utopian Esperanto from the outset and multiplied world English in

---

7. See Luigi Bonaffini, *Dialect Poetry of Southern Italy* (New York: Legas Publishing, 1997); Francesco Granatiero, *Dal Gargano all'Appennino, le voci in dialetto* (Foggia: Sentieri Meridiani, 2012), and P. V. Mengaldo, *Poeti italiani del novecento* (Milano: Mondadori, 1998).

the space of decades to world Englishes. Pascoli's outlook is in no way
a *fin de siècle* literary decadence—a falling-off—but a prescription for
Orphic descent into the depths of language, our mythic origins, at times
"agrammatical and pre-grammatical." He believed this dead language, this
Ur-language, would give us new life.

   Pascoli is also aware of the demands an emerging modern world's
mobility will make upon language. "Italy" (this is the *Italian*-language poem's
title), the last poem of his *Primi poemetti*, describes an American-born Italian
eight-year-old's return to her ancestral land. The poem ends with her about
to board a ship for her return to Cincinnati:

> *Sweet sweet... era un sussurro senza fine*
> *nel cielo azzurro. Rosea, bionda, e mesta,*
> *Molly era in mezzo ai bimbi e alle bambine.*
>
> *Il nonno, solo, in là volgea la testa*
> *bianca. Sonava intorno mezzodì.*
> *Chiedono i bimbi con vocìo di festa:*
>
> *"Tornerai, Molly ?" Rispondeva: — Sì! —*

Sweet Sweet... It was an endless whisper
in the blue sky. Redhead, blond, and sad
Molly stood among the children and babies.

The grandfather alone turns his white head
away. Midday rings.
The children ask with festive voice

Molly, will you return? She answered, *Sì!*

Benedetto Croce calls the poem *orrida* (horrid), but from a century's distance, one can more sympathetically see Pascoli as among the first to address a human struggle more urgent than ever in our own day.[8] The "dead language" attunes him to the living reality: Aeneas after all was an exile, and Virgil the poet of nationhood paradoxically also a poet of exile. And Dante, of course, exiled from his native Florence, embodied an age of spiritual homesickness. Pascoli reinvigorates the classical themes of exile and the medieval pilgrimage. Four of his collections contain poems about emigration: "The Hammerless Gun" in *Canti del Castelvecchio;* "Italy" in *Primi Poemetti;* "Gli emigranti nella luna" in *Nuovi Poemetti;* and in 1911, he wrote "Inno degli emigranti Italiani," "Hymn to the Italian Emigrants," for the Italian community in New York. It was set to music and sung at the dedication of the Dante memorial there.

Such an immersion in the nature of language also accounts for the scientific precision with which he writes about the natural world. In section xiv of his *Fanciullino*, Pascoli notes we should distinguish between a "hillside covered with marguerites and a field full of crocuses." In his quest for a precise and common language, one can see an antecedent to Pound's imagism ("To use the language of common speech, but to employ the exact word, not the nearly exact, nor the merely decorative word"). Gianfranca Lavezzi's Italian edition of *Myricae* includes an illustrated botanical appendix, as essential to a reading of the poems as an index of his references to the classics. For Pascoli, it is no paradox that human *civilization* is part of a larger *natural* world.

For readers today, Pascoli can serve as a psychopomp—someone who leads us through a world that is both lost and coming to be, and above all he can be one who shows us that this condition pertains not just to his *fin-de-siècle* times but to our own post-millennial ones as well. We see this clearly in a late essay, *L'Era Nuova*, published in 1900, in which the poet reflects upon the advances of science and the diminishment of the spiritual life they apparently wrought. Despite the wealth of religious iconography and tropes

8. Benedetto Croce, *Giovanni Pascoli: Studio Critico* (Bari: Gius, Laterza & Figli, 1920), 46.

in his poetry, Pascoli was himself not a believer. As Lisa Barca shows, the poet saw that the contribution of science to spiritual life is precisely that it can make no contribution. It can only reveal our final destiny more clearly: We die. And so he writes in a moment that can only be seen as prophetic:

> *Se io sapessi descrivervi la sensazione del nulla, io sarei un poeta di quelli non ancor nati o non ancor parlanti.*[9]

> If I could describe the sensation of nothingness, I would be among those poets not yet born or not yet able to speak.

The line to Ungaretti's poetry of the first World War and to the existential gulf that followed the second could not be clearer. The poet of myth has become the poet of existence; where history has been destroyed, poetry remains.

Maria Truglio's *Beyond the Family Romance: The Legend of Pascoli* (Toronto: University of Toronto Italian Studies, 2007) is the most important study of the poet in English.

Rosamaria LaValva's *The Eternal Child: The Poetry and Poetics of Giovanni Pascoli* (Chapel Hill: *Annali d'italianistica*, 1999) is a valuable work that should be more widely available. Directed to a non-academic audience, my version aspires to be somewhat more colloquial. For instance, LaValva renders Pascoli's key neologism *gloriola* as "petty fame." This is accurate, but hardly cutting in the way Pascoli intends. Unhappy changes to mass culture since the beginnings of the *American Poetry Review* and *People* magazine have given us a precise equivalent in *celebrity*. Pascoli's revulsion at such builds on Leopardi's (whom he quotes) and looks back though a tradition of its own to Petronius.

---

9. Giovanni Pascoli, *Pensieri E Discorsi* (Bologna: Nicola Zanichelli, 1907), 152.

Our poet of the doorway stands appropriately as the first figure in Geoffrey Brock's *Farrar Straus & Giroux Book of Twentieth-Century Italian Poetry* (New York: Farrar Strauss and Giroux, 2012) and he is the opening poet in Ned Condini and Dana Renga's *An Anthology of Modern Italian Poetry: In English Translation, with Italian Texts* (New York: Modern Language Association, 2009). Taije Silverman with Marina Della Putta Johnston's *Selected Poems of Giovanni Pascoli* (Princeton, 2019) appeared while this manuscript was in the late stages of preparation. It is certain to be a central contribution to Pascoli studies. Important translations of individual poems, notably by Patrick Bannon, Gregory Dowling, and Maria Truglio, have appeared in journals. P. R. Horne's *Selected Poems* of Giovanni Pascoli (Manchester: Manchester University Press, 1983) was the first book-length collection of Pascoli's poetry, followed by Deborah Brown, Richard Jackson, and Susan Thomas's very fine *Last Voyage* (Pasadena: Red Hen Press, 2010).

There are several online Italian-language resources for Pascoli's writing, notably the *Pascoli Foundation* (www.fondazionepascoli.it/2014/Index.html) and *Biblioteca della Letteratura Italiana* (http://www.letteraturaitaliana.net/autori/pascoli_giovanni.html). The translator is particularly informed by Giorgio Agamben's essay on *Pascoli e il pensiero della voce*, contained in the nottetempo edition of *Il fanciullino* (Rome, 2012). Gianfranca Lavezzi's edition of *Myricae* (Milan: BUR Rizzoli, 2015) is indispensible for its textual apparatus, as is Giuseppe Nava's edition of *Canti di castelvecchio* (Milan: BUR Rizzoli, 2014). Luigi Oliveto's *Giovanni Pascoli, il poeta delle cose* (Primamedia Editore, 2012) is a useful critical biography, and Giovanni Caserta's *Giovanni Pascoli a Matera* (Venoza: Osanna Edizione, 2013) offers detail into the poet's early teaching experience there.

My work here follows gratefully on all these others. Any shortcomings are of course entirely my own.

, É' tard,

irelo;

ic che guard

llo stelo;

yolg

II. O LITTLE ONE

Il fanciullino

I

There's a little child in us who doesn't just shake with fear, as Cebes the Theban thought (who first noticed this little one in himself), but also cries and exults.[1]* When we are still of tender age, this little one mingles his voice with ours, and the two of us romp and wrestle—together always—and whether they fear, hope, enjoy, or cry, there's a single shudder, shout, or cry. But then we grow up, and he stays small. New desires flare up in us, but he remains fixed in his ancient serene state of wonder; our voice deepens, but he still hears and makes others hear his tinkling, bell-chime voice. Adulthood consumes us with arguing and advancing our own pursuits, and we no longer feel the secret tingling of childhood so keenly. We pay less attention to the corner of the soul where that other voice resonates. And the invisible child is lost to the adolescent, as not to a self-aware man or an old one, because the young man—unlike the old—sees the child as unlike him. The young man rarely and only fugitively has anything to do with the child; he disdains that other's conversation, as if he were embarrassed by a past so near. But a man at rest loves talking to the child, hearing his chatter, and responding sincerely and seriously. The harmony of their voices is as sweet to the listener's ear as the warble of a nightingale by a murmuring stream.

Or at the ancient gray sea. The sea is weary with life's stress and covers itself with white spume and the beach with death rattles. Still, between one wave and the next, the singular notes of the nightingale arise, now full of lamentation, now jubilant, now questioning. The nightingale is as small as the sea is huge, as young as the latter is old. The bard is old and his ode is young. Väinämöinen is old and projects a new song.[2] Who can imagine the bard, that singer of epics, as other than old? Old with repentance, Vyasa knows all things sacred and profane. Ossian is old—as are all the Skaldic poets.

*Please see endnotes for this essay.

The bard is one who has seen (*oîde*) and therefore knows, and sometimes sees no more: He is the clairvoyant (*aoidós*) who makes his song appear.[3]

Old age doesn't prevent us from hearing the inner child's voice; on the contrary, beyond the ferment in which young men drown, old age invites us into the soul's penumbra.[4] And if his outer eyes see no more, well, then the old man just sees with those great inner eyes, and has nothing before him but the vision that he had as a child and that all children have. And so, if one wants to portray Homer, one paints him as old and blind, with a child leading him by the hand, always looking all around and speaking. By a little boy or girl, by the god or goddess; the god who sowed all those songs in anticipation of Phemius, or the goddess to whom the blind bard of Achilles and Odysseus turned.[5]

II

But the chattering brat or the voluble virgin dwelt invisibly in him. They were
his very childhood, preserved in his heart throughout life, and resurrected
to remember and sing after the great ferment of the senses. His boyhood
therefore speaks more of Achilles than of Helen, and lingers over the Cyclops
rather than Calypso. The child doesn't care about the love of women, however
beautiful and divine, but about bronze spears and war chariots, long voyages,
and great misfortunes. And so the child that lives in ancient Homer dwells on
these things, rather than the beauty of Castor and Pollux, the voluptuousness
of the night's goddess, or the daughter of the sun.[6] And he speaks in his
properly childish language.

He returns from countries no more distant than the village is to mountain
shepherds, but reveals things to children who've never been. He recounts at
length, heatedly, one particular after another, leaving out no detail — branches
for the fire are, for example, leafless. For everything looks new and beautiful
to him — even that which he has already seen — and he believes they should
look new and beautiful to his listeners. "Beautiful" and "huge" recur constantly
in his telling and he always adds the noteworthy detail. His ships are black,
their prows brightly painted; they float well balanced, have beautiful
instruments, beautiful benches; the sea is colorful and always tumbling,
salty, and foaming. The warriors? — They have long hair. Their helmets? —
They have crests that sway with each step. Their spears? — They cast long
shadows. In order not to be misunderstood, he repeats the same thought in
different ways: He says "*A little, hardly much,*" "*To live, hardly to die!,*" "*He spoke and
said,*" "*They gathered and were all in one place.*"

He has plenty of expressions that bring us up short: "*Obey, because to obey . . . is
better.*" "*I alone should remain without a gift? That's not right!*" Things can never be too
clear: "*There were eight small hens, nine with the mother who had hatched them.*" "*Ajax, that small
one, not huge like the other, but very much smaller: He was small . . .*" Sometimes he can be

17

sublime, but without calculation: He imbues the circumstance with greater meaning and sense. A divine archer draws back the bow, "*and all they could see were flaming heaps of the dead.*" The supreme deity raises his brow, tosses his head, and "*Olympus shook, who is so grand.*" Above all, in order to make himself completely understood with regard to something new and strange, he draws his likenesses from the experiences of his listeners. And in this he has two contrary modes: Now he calls up a little thing to have one understand something big, now a major thing to make one see something minor. To depict the onslaught of a mob, he summons up a stormy sea hurling itself against the shore with huge foaming waves, shouting, and thunder; a swarm of flies around buckets full of milk evokes the vast confusion of an army.

This was his only artifice, if one can even call it artifice to innocently cast something in smaller yet clearer terms, as when he compared the liquid speech of aged wise men to the rasping of cicadas, or a great hero's fortitude to the indifference of an ass that continues to fill itself in a field while children try to drive it along with a beating. No, no, the blind man's child doesn't want to win honor for himself so much as he wants to make himself understood. He doesn't exaggerate since the facts he relates seemed marvelous to him just as they were, seemed so in the soul of all his listeners. Now as then, they listen with amazement. And it wouldn't be reasonable to believe that things could be more realistic after thirty centuries. Even after thirty centuries men aren't born thirty years old, and even after thirty years they still remain children in part.

III

But is this musical child really in us all? I wouldn't want to think there's anyone he doesn't dwell in, such would that person's misery and solitude seem to me. Then, he wouldn't have that shallow breast from which the voices of other people echo, and nothing of his soul would reach the souls of his peers. He wouldn't be bound to all humanity, except for those chains of the law, that either oppress him or that he bears lightly, either a slave indifferent by habit or a rebel against the novel imposition. Because people do not feel themselves to be brothers, everyone arms himself for the battle of life—though we grow up differently and take up different weapons—and the Little One in each of us seeks out another for the least bit of comfort and peace, for an embrace, and for play.

Still, some say there are only two kinds of people, those who do not see there are two, and those who see one kind set indistinguishably against the other, like a sweet current in the bitter sea. They even live in the same family, under the eyes of the same mother and live the same life to all appearances, born of the same seed in a single womb; and one kind of person is utterly strange to the other, not just with respect to their experience of one tract of sky and earth but to how each sees all humanity and nature itself. They might call each other by name, but they will never know each other. And the reason for this is that the one person has the eternal child in himself, and the other—unhappy one!—doesn't.

But I don't like to believe in such unhappiness: that this child should seem absent in some, and that others don't accept his presence, or believe he's just an illusion. Perhaps people expect who-knows-what miracles and achievements from him; and because they don't see such things in themselves or others, they decide that he doesn't exist. But the signs of his presence and the acts of his life are simple and humble. He is afraid of the dark, because he sees or believes he sees in the dark; he dreams in the light or seems to dream, remembering things never seen. He is the one who talks to the animals, to the trees, to the stones, to the clouds, to the stars, who populates the shade with ghosts and heaven with gods.[7] He cries and laughs without reason at things that escape our senses and our reason. At the death of the beloved, he is the one who rises to say the childish thing that dissolves us in tears and that saves us.[8] Mad with joy, he thoughtlessly throws out the serious word that restrains us. He makes both happiness and misadventure tolerable, tempering them with bitterness and sweetness equally soft in memory. He humanizes love and caresses one like a sister (Oh! The whispering of two children among the sounds of beasts), caresses and consoles the girl in the woman. In the serious man, he stands ready to listen with admiration to tales and legends; in the peaceful man he evokes a shrill fanfare of trumpets and echo of bagpipes; and in a corner of the nonbeliever's soul, he wafts incense from the altar that he has preserved from time immemorial. He makes us lose track of time, when we are going about our affairs—for now he wants to stop to watch the titmouse sing, and now gather sweet flowers, and now strike sparks from a flint. He chatters ceaselessly; and without him we would never see anything out of the ordinary. Without him, we wouldn't think of and smile at these things, for he is the Adam who names all that he sees and feels, discovering ingenious resemblances and relations among things, adapting the name of the greatest to the smallest, and the contrary. Astonishment drives him more than ignorance; curiosity more than loquacity. He shrinks things in order to see them clearly; he magnifies them for our admiration. His language isn't flawed like those who only go halfway, but prodigious, like one who'd give two thoughts to one word. And to all things he gives a sign, a sound, a color, so that he can recognize forever that which he sees a single time.

Is there anyone who hasn't felt all this? Perhaps the child is quiet in you, Professor, because you frown too much; and you don't hear him, Mr. Banker, in your invisible and assiduous counting. He makes you pout, O Peasant, as you dig and plow unable to stop and look around a little. And you, O Worker, he sleeps with closed fists in you, shut up all day in your sunless, noisy office.

But I want to believe he is in all.

Let them be workers, peasants, bankers, and professors at church on a feast day; or poor and rich finding themselves exasperated or bored by a musical performance at the theater: There are children at the window of those souls, illuminated by a smile or soaked by a tear that burns in the eyes of their unknowing hosts; here are the little ones who know one another whether at the hovel's tattered curtains or palace's balcony, contemplating a common memory and dream.

IV

As with all others, so with me. And because of our time together as children, I haven't lived a life defined only by pain (and there was much pain)—I've almost never lost sight of or failed to hear him. To the contrary, not having lost those first affections, I sometimes wonder how much I've "experienced." And the one *I* says yes, because there is more life where there is less death, and that other *I* says no because he believes the opposite. In any case, I often speak with him, as he speaks sometimes with me, and I tell him: Little boy, you don't know how to think except in your own childish way—profoundly, because all at once—without descending the steps of thought one by one— we're transported into the abyss of truth. . . .

Oh! I can't believe that certain lines of logic can come from you, simple child, even when expressed in a language like yours and rendered in your rhythms! Perhaps those rhythms make the logic easier to follow, and your words are easier to understand; or maybe not, since your leaps distract us by dazzling, and your words draw us close, cradling us; so that the thinker's goal can't be reached as it would without those images and without that cadence. But say it's so: I don't believe it's ever your goal to have someone say, *You've convinced me of something that I hadn't thought of.* And even less: *You have persuaded me of something against my will.* You don't propose much, Little One. In your frank and simple way, you say what you see and feel, limpidly, immediately, and you stand by your words, when one who hears you exclaims: *I see, too, now, now. I hear what you're saying, and what was, surely, also within and without me before, and I didn't understand, or not so well as* now!

This is all you want, beyond the delight you yourself retain of that vision and feeling. And how could you aspire to such grand works with such small instruments? Because you won't let yourself be seduced by a certain similarity, for example, between your language and that of orators. Yes: Orators also magnify or diminish what they please, and they use a word that *paints* instead

22

of one that *points* as it suits them. But the difference is that they do what they please when they please.

You?—No, Little One: You always say what you see, the way you see it. *They* do so at their peril, but you wouldn't know how to speak otherwise; orators speak differently from those who really know. You illuminate the thing; they dazzle the eye. You want one to see better; they want one not to see at all. In sum, theirs is the liar's artifice, stealing the will of those less clever. Yours is the native tongue of the innocent child, who, exultant or lamenting, speaks to other innocent children.

Isn't it so? . . .

Thus, Little One, you can only think in your own way, sometimes the most common and sometimes sublime, clear and unexpected. You can do this for the one closest to you: You utter my meaning and I speak your thought. I'm telling you this with more than my customary seriousness, and I want an answer from you less . . . how should I say this? Infantile? . . . poetic, *unadorned*.

V

You know that I love you, my intimate benefactor, invisible cup bearer of the *nepenthe* and *ácholon*, dispelling sorrow and anger, thou troubadour and guardian of a secret treasure of tears and smiles![9] And still, you know that I no longer think of you as an irrational boy, nor deem it a waste of time to listen when you speak within. Oh! We're very different. You sometimes encounter the rigmarole of isosyllabic and homeoteleuton (don't be afraid!—these are, as they say, "figures of speech")[10] with which certain ear-men would have us believe they are making your art, but I too sometimes find such cadences and sonorities neither natural nor sensible. But that's one moment. I forget the jargon and then, I tell you, you fix me between fear and discontent with eyes full of wonder. I tell you:

No, no, don't be afraid. You are the eternal child who marvels at everything, all there is, as if for the first time. The adult doesn't see the interior world or the outer one as you do: He knows many particulars that you don't. He has studied and has made the work of others his own. Thus, the adult of our times knows more than past times, and bit by bit climbs, higher and always higher. The first people didn't know a thing—they knew what you know, Little One.

Surely they resemble you, because their person was, so to speak, interfused with the inner child. They marveled, with all their undefined being, at everything; all was truly new then, not only for the child but for the man. They marveled with a feeling mixed now with joy, now with sadness, now with hope, now with fear. If they later wanted to express this commotion to themselves and others, they drew from the quiver those precious and numerous arrows, without having to shoot.

Those first people spoke with uniform reserve and measured gravity the difficult word that astonished them, that flew and shone and sounded and was them and became others and returned to the soul from which it had gone forth after long meditative silence. Oh! They didn't throw them out like cheap baubles had in abundance, those new-born words resting in soft nests, marked with the most vital impressions, worked with more ingenious alloys! They felt all the merits, the weight and the stamp of their metal, and the sound which broke from lips in the beginning and resonated in open ears at the end. Now you, little one, do as they did, because you are like them.

You do like all the children who not only play and leap with their well-rhymed songs when they're old enough, but also when as babes they make the woods ring with their babbling strings of *pa pa* and *ma ma.*

And this makes sense because it is natural. You are still in the presence of the new world and endeavor to give meaning to the new word. The world is born again for every one born into the world, and the mystery of your being and function is this: You are primordial, O Little One, and the world that you see anew is the primordial one. The rhythm (not this or that one but rhythm in general) with which you, in your way, sway or dance, is *primordial.* What fools they are who want to rebel against one or the other of these two necessities that only apparently clash: to see the new and to see the old; and to say that which has never been said, and to say it as that which has always been and will be said!

And they object—some with the foul gesture of pedants: Y*ou don't see this metaphor in* [insert the name of a more-or-less recent poet]—others with the arrogant pose of "innovators": *This isn't anything new!* In general, the old take old age as the ultimate authority; and the young imagine every strength lies in youth. One's as bad as the other; for the vaunting of one is always impertinent and the other is never without sorrow. And whereas the old can't make out the child's acute chattering because of their senile deafness, the miserable vanity of the young man's *I* shuts it out. In truth those young men aren't really young—if they were, they wouldn't notice themselves. And realizing one has grown old, he dresses up, colors his hair and shouts at the young. And isn't that the case for all you old croakers?

In any case, Peace! Know that for poetry, youth isn't enough; it takes childhood!

VI

You're wise, and I'm glad. You don't want to repeat what's already been said
or to summon up the unsayable; you don't want to be useless or vain. You
want what's new, but you know that the new resides in things, for one who
knows how to see, and you don't work yourself up to be bewitching and
sophisticated. One doesn't invent the new, one discovers it. So I'm glad,
speaking between us, I mean, within myself ... but we understand each other
right away: I don't heap great praises on you because I don't see great reason
to. How's that? Wait and be patient—I'll come to it at length. First I have to
ask—Do you have a goal? (Beyond, I mean, precisely what to say or do?)
Tell me—I need to know.—You don't answer?—Are you thinking? Hesitating?
Doubting?—I guess you're not planning to help out your aged host with a
bit of that gold he could really use. Indeed, I imagine you only know about
metaphoric gold, which can't be spent? Do you laugh? Let's understand each
other. I know for certain that you wouldn't think of straight-out giving
me anything useful, but I suspect you're thinking to provide it indirectly,
bestowing I wouldn't know what favor on my poor person and what gift to
my humble virtue, except industriousness, since you know that I work and
could profit from more. Well, you'd be deceiving yourself. You know it's just
the opposite, and reasonably so: You are a child. Now these days not everyone
knows how to distinguish you, the child, from me, the old man, and because
others hear and see me act like a child sometimes, they think that I always
play the child, even when I'm seriously at work making a living. For this
reason they hold my serious work in less esteem, and I earn less. And they are
wrong. Always? You know they're not always wrong.

They're right, for example (and I'm not just speaking of myself but of many
others) when among my thoughts that would not be otherwise than clear and
correct, they see something like your smiles and shouts. Sparrows may be
graceful birds (they, too: and why not?) but peasants don't want them around

26

while they're sowing their fields, however graceful they might be. Gladioli are beautiful flowers, but it's much better if they don't get in the grain. They're beautiful to look at—I don't deny that they might delight people, but not those who hope to use the grain, you understand? Likewise, when the conversation has to get serious, your fluttering wings and eyes can't help but displease.

And do you know what happens? Finding you so far out of place, they don't think that you're a silver-throated child but a hoarse old man, a man full of lies: and they shout *Rhetoric!* Now, to avoid such a mixup with you and such damage to me, it wouldn't be bad if I minded my own business, went off and slept under the fragrant marjoram in deep *Idalian* woods. If you knew Plato, I would tell you how he was right in asserting that poets create *mythos* and not *logos*, fables and not reasonable arguments.¹¹ I'm not wrong in asserting that reasoners make *logos* and not *mythos*. But it's rather difficult to find one who contents himself with only doing what he must. And Plato himself . . . But he was Plato.

Turning to us, then, I don't get anything useful from you, O Little One, either directly or indirectly. Whatever you might say, nothing. Indeed whatever might it be? Speak!

VII

THE LITTLE BOY

I don't give jewels or gold to you
O sweet guest; it's true;
But I see to it that you have enough of those flowers
That you gather from the green path,
From the wall, from the damp cracks
From the sharp hedge.

I don't bring a steaming roast of veal
to your table, but I cook up
the radicchio,
Not without your burnet,
With an egg from the hen
That cried out to you in the morning.

You don't plow for me, O poet,
neither rocky vineyards, nor thick
fallow fields; but tell me what gladdens
the sullen lord more —
vineyards and fields
or the chatty sparrow and you!

It's not fragile porcelain cups,
the radiant golden lamp that brightens you
but your beloved rough kitchen
and well-stocked cupboard;
you love the flame that glows
from its sharp branches.

You've only got what hangs by a thread,
no valet, no pretty maid,
but happy, grateful housework
done by your sweet sister
who ties her apron and smiles
ties it and sits down

with you ... and on the deathbed
that's rough and hard for all
what can I give you, do you know?
O deathbed rose, fallen
from the thorns; what sweet
sorrow there was!

VIII

Good! You've sung and spoken your stanzas and your truth. And it occurs to me that beyond this truth, let's say, of which I am usually witness, there is an undercurrent of truth more condensed and less common, to which the conscience of all responds with immediate assent. What? That poetry insofar as it is poetry—poetry without an adjective before it, has a supreme moral and social utility. And you've never had to explain your goal to me: You've just said what you see and hear, and in doing so expressed the fitting end of poetry. Now it seems to me, if one thinks about it, that this poetic feeling is what satisfies the shepherd in his hut, the bourgeois in his apartment furnished without good taste but with patience and diligence. That's what you're saying.

Or is it the contrary?—The shepherd neglecting his sheep, daydreams of a startup shop in the nearby town; the bourgeois fantasies a palace in the great and roaring city. Are people such as these fantasists and dreamers the poets and not the others? For me, though, the poetic feeling is one thing, fantasy another, and they can be inspired and animated by poetic feeling or not. Poetry discovers—do I have to say it?—the smiles and tears in things, and these are made of two infant eyes that simply and serenely watch within the obscure tumult of our soul.

At times, not seeing anything luminous or beautiful in what's around them, they shut themselves off and dream, gazing into the distance. But what they're looking for lies simply in the things around them, and not having found them, it's not their poetry that's defective, but their eyesight.—Are you saying (I'm not speaking of you, now, O Little One, but of overgrown children), are you saying that the poetic feeling abounds most in one who, twisting his eyes away from present reality only finds beautiful and worthy things for poetry in the flowers of American agave, or who admires and makes others admire the small grayish-pink tassels of the pimpernel above a chasm? I don't want to say that one doesn't find any poetry in the science and fantasy that make such things justifiably admirable; but the more clever it is, the more quickly it bores the reader, and in any case, inasmuch as the absent things or those never seen, are always marvelous to all, such a poet pretends to have stirred the audience when he has simply gotten them drunk. He has been perhaps witty and convivial, but one whose words stir without guile, without need of goblets, has greater merit.

Now therefore one finds the poetic feeling in that which surrounds one, that others disparage, who can't find it under their feet and must look for it elsewhere. And that feeling is a consummate blessing that softly and gently stops the unquenchable desire forever pushing unhappy anxiety-ridden people down the road toward happiness. Oh! That one might know how to strengthen this feeling in those who have it, forestall its loss in those who are about to lose it, instill it again into those who lack it — wouldn't one who knew how to do that accomplish more for human life than any so-clever troubadour of comfort and medicine? I can't say how much the communion of people would be advantaged; especially in these times in which the road toward impossible happiness is regarded with such glaring contempt in those who go on, and such desperate envy in those who remain behind. Already in other times a Poet (I'm not even worthy to pronounce your holy name, O Parthenias![12]) saw the dancers spinning dizzily in the vain circle of passion — those times were like these — and the world's conflagration in a war of all against all and each for himself flickers on the horizon. *That* Poet knew the cithara of Orpheus was still more potent than the club of Hercules over the proud and monstrous. And he made poetry without thinking of anything else, without putting on the airs of an adviser, an oracle, a prophet of good and evil auguries: He sang to sing. And I don't know how to measure what the effects of his song were, but it was great, for sure, and has lasted to this day, pulsating with sweetness in our unquiet souls.

O dilettantes of grandstand phrases, o versifiers of social theory, you who currently snub all poetry except your own, who, one wants to say, sniff at *POETRY*, tell me: Wasn't the poet of the *Georgics* at home in the century of

Augustus? Yes, isn't it true? He taught us how to love life without spectacle—either the painful spectacle of misery or the envious one of wealth. He wanted to abolish the struggle between class and war among people. What do you want, O Socialist poets, who say such different things and speak so differently from him?

IX

Of two fraternal poets of the age of Augustus (since one cannot speak of Virgil without adding Horace) it is said that philosophy led them to their sane and pious view of society and life. But no: it was the Little One who led them by the hand, saying: I will lead you where poetry and truth can be found at the same time. It was the little child, if anyone, who enabled their feelings to transcend philosophy.

Consider: Cato and Varro wrote about agriculture before Virgil. They were men of great judgment and knowledge. Cato, for example, describing the duties of the paterfamilias, advises: "Sell oil, if it sells well; wine, surplus grain, sell it. The unneutered oxen, the mediocre stud-mares, likewise the sheep, the wool, the skins, an old cart, old iron tools, an elderly slave, a sick slave, and other things in excess—sell them. A head of house should turn to selling, not buying."[13] Numbering slaves among rusted scrap iron and other old things unsettles us; but it was natural then to include them in such a list. Indeed, Varro elegantly categorizes instruments used in agriculture: "Other things should be divided into three groups: vocal, semi-vocal and mute— slaves are vocal; semi-vocal includes cattle; carriages are mute."[14] It could only be expected, that Virgil writing about agriculture in verse—*in verse*— not in fantasy, but having studied the arguments of other books, would have spoken not just of wagons and cattle but also of slaves, who were the principal instruments of cultivation. For example, we must expect him to instruct us in offering flowering grasses and provender to breed-foals,[15] and to the tame steers not only grass under the willows and reed-tops from marshes, but also young wheat picked by hand;[16] and further to teach the good steward about bread and what goes with it, wine and clothes, and how to form a family. Speaking of olives, it's certain that he will think of *Pulmentarium familiae* (food families). The great teacher Cato simply says: "Sweeten the olives in the casks as much as you can. For olives are also good that only yield a little oil.

Sweeten them and be very sparing, so that it lasts as long as possible. When olives are to be eaten, use vinegar."[17] He did well, it seems to me, instructing that the residue of olive pressing should be given to the slaves. As to their woolen clothes falling to pieces, he also wisely tells us: "When you give a new tunic or overcoat to a slave, first take the old one to make patches." In short, a poet who knows how to speak with solemnity and gravity of humble things can offer these and similar providences in beautiful and decorous verse.

Oh! Yes! There are no slaves in Virgil. You never find the word *servus* in his poems: "Handmaid" occurs twice, and with reference to other times and customs,[18] where the poet knows very well that kings were served by many, but even then he calls them *famuli* (servants) and *ministri* (agents), not *slaves*.[19] His fields, though, those he taught us how to cultivate, those that he plowed and seeded with his sweet verses, those didn't have people in chains and shackles. The poet, who in his first eclogue assumes the persona of a freed slave, has proclaimed to his Italic companions the word that Tityrus voices so strongly: LIBERTAS.[20] Virgil's farmers are neither slaves nor hired hands. They are those of whom Varro speaks,[21] that cultivate the earth on their own, like an alliance of small-holders and their offspring. Virgil has this in mind when he exclaims that they would be happy if they could know their happiness, with such peace, such fruitfulness, among such beauty without the afflictions of misery or being overseen, working in their seasons, enjoying the family at home and the dear festivals outside.[22] Of people who work for others, never a trace.

The poet's ideal is that little old man Cilice, transplanted from his fatherland into the neighborhood of Taranto. He had a few plots of land good for neither grain nor pasture nor vineyard: a house for crickets. Now this capable old man had a garden, not just with cabbages but also lilies and roses, and fruit trees and bee-hives and a greenhouse.[23] Yes: the two great poets dreamed of the small and modest. Virgil said: *Praise the big field, and keep the small one.*[24] And Horace: *This was my prayer: a little field not too big, with a garden, a fountain and also a little woods.*[25] Who wouldn't prefer a big field to the small if he didn't have to cultivate it himself? But for two poets, when they were poets it wasn't so simple. To put it better: The child that was in them preferred like all children that which is small: the pony, the small carriage, the small flower-bed. Oh, is there anyone who grudges Horace this love of the mean! But to be a poet of the mean isn't to be a mediocre poet—just the opposite. One who says he'd love a seraglio of women doesn't know how to love. He isn't a poet who isn't fixed in a vision his eyes can test.

And the grand things, the costly things, the sublime things don't rise to poetry if they aren't felt and described in person by one astonished in their presence, exactly because he is small, poor, humble. The poet is humanity's pauper, and he's often blind and old. And if he doesn't seem so, if on the other hand he is a great lord and a youth and happy, well, that means that he's a little pauper despite his wealth, because of the Little One within; that is to say—he has stayed poor as a boy. The child is always poor, even if born in a golden cradle, and puts his hand to everything and everyone as if he hadn't anything and wanted hard, common bread and wanted the hard work of his troubled countryside.

This is why the child Virgil bore in his heart didn't want slaves in the fields. Will we tell ourselves that Virgil drew this law of liberty from some philosopher's books or some prophet? No: He himself was perhaps unaware he proclaimed this liberty. His poetry abolished slavery because servitude wasn't poetic.

If it wasn't poetic, and the divine child hadn't known what is not poetic, he wouldn't have seen it. In any case, if we had no testimony other than Virgil's from his time, we would have to believe that the misery and shame of our own time, of all time, didn't exist in his. O, we would have to believe that Christ, who hadn't yet been born, inspired the peasant poet of Hesperia as a presentiment of great human fraternity, as a *viaticum* of his coming! There isn't slavery in Virgilian Italy; neither is there the wage-slave, neither the sharecropper!

X

Thus not deliberately and without straying off, as Dante puts it: the true poet *carries the torch behind*, not *before*—or rather *within* him, within the dear soul—the splendor and ardor of poetry's torch.[26] He is, as they say today, *socialist*, or as they might say, *human*. Thus the poem, not tuned to anything but poetry, is that which betters and regenerates humanity not deliberately excluding evil, but naturally that which is *unpoetic*. Now one gradually finds that the unpoetic is that which morality recognizes as evil and that aesthetics declares ugly. But it isn't hoary philosophy that determines what is evil and ugly. It's the inner child who feels revulsion—the one who while narrating the exploits of his heroes, and telling all about them, describing their meals and nights following their battles, and their speeches, and showing us their horses, for example, how they grazed, sweated and foamed, not that they were put to stable, just don't ever say (you see that I take what I can, so you don't hold your nose) don't ever say that they pissed; thus our soul only relates of the good and our vision recalls only the beautiful. For singing of evil demands continuous effort, if it's not to sound mad. And in this case, madness is exactly this, thinking of the good and singing of evil.

Therefore, dear Little One, although you don't see anything but the good, they are really wrong who claim to find anything of merit in your host. Even a gangster can have a child in him who sings the delights of peace and innocence and the house where he can't live anymore and the church where he no longer knows how to pray.

XI

The poet, when he really is a poet, which simply means that the boy has spoken within, is thereby the true inspiration of good and civil customs, of love of country, kin, and others. Thus in belief and deed, the sound of the harp gathers stones to make the city walls, brings plants to life, and tames the beasts of the primordial forest. Singers guide and educate the people. Stones, plants, beasts, and first people follow the voice of an eternal child, of a young god, the smallest and most gentle there is in the savage tribe. These, in truth, civilized themselves contemplating, and listening to their infancy.

Thus in his fierce times, Homer finds in Achilles—the fiercest of the heroes, which is to say most true and poetic—a type of such moral perfection, that he could serve as a model to Socrates, when he chose death over evil. So Virgil, fixing his gaze solely on the poetic in more gentle times, reveals to us the long-awaited vision of—oh my!—a humanity, good, happy at work and with the simple joy of sons without war and without slaves. It seems that the people of his time prayed for that still-unfulfilled desire of our own workers: eight hours of work, eight for sleep, and a third eight for diversion. O! Sometimes in Virgil, the peasant adds night to the days work!—Yes, but what sweetness of work for the man who is his own master, turning pine branches into torches, and the woman who spins her web or stirs her cauldron singing.[27] In the *Aeneid*, Virgil sings of war and battles, but all the sense of epic marvel lies in the morning chirping of swallows or those sparrows that awakens Evander in his tent, where the imperial palaces of Rome would rise![28]

But Homer and Virgil did not do this with calculation.

And the poet must not do it so. The poet is a poet, not an orator or preacher, not a philosopher, historian, teacher, tribune, or demagogue, not a creature of state or court. And neither is he (*pace*, my Teacher) an artisan who shapes sword, shield, and plowshare, or (*pace*, many others) a goldsmith or refiner of gold that others provide. Feeling and vision matter infinitely more to the makeup of a poet than the manner in which he passes them on to others. Indeed, when he transmits things, even though standing before an audience, he speaks rather more to himself than to them. He doesn't seem to be aware of the audience. He speaks strongly (but not too!) better to hear himself than to be understood by someone else. To use images that are present now to my spirit, however much saying so displeases, he is a greengrocer; a greengrocer, yes, or a gardener, who sprouts and grows flowers or cauliflower. Do you know what he isn't? He isn't a chef, and he isn't a florist who serves cauliflowers in beautiful plates with good sauces, with the flowers arranged in bunches or garlands. All he knows is how to pull scarred or withered leaves from the cabbage, and tie up flowers the best way with willow stems, which is to say that he unifies his thoughts with that native rhythm that is in the soul of the nursing infant and the ragamuffin at play.

Now can this poet also be a civic and social prophet?

Only without intending to be, if ever.

One finds him in the crowd, watching the banners pass and the trumpets sound. He throws out his words, which scarcely has he pronounced them, others hear as if they themselves had spoken. And one finds him again in that crowd watching the possessions of a poor family thrown into the street. He says the word, and one immediately sees the eyes of all fill with tears.

The poet expresses the word that all have on tip of the tongue but none has spoken. But he isn't that one who climbs on a chair or table in order to harangue. He doesn't lead away but is borne along; he doesn't persuade but is convinced.

Because he thinks of country and society there comes a moment when everyone around thinks of him. If not, it's a serious misfortune. Our most gentle feeling is for our mother. But what would you say of one who chronicled his mother's every moment? "This morning she rose, dear mother! I've watched her, poor mother! Poor dear mother has given me my coffee and milk!"—Such a man is either an imbecile, or he's pretending, putting on airs of loving that which is so easy to love! *Oh! Mother is ill; mother is far away; mother is dead!* So then we think of mother and pine. Or mother receives a great consolation and we are more than consoled: We are seized by song's impulse.

So, too, with the country. We only think of it at festivals or at its—*our!*—times of disgrace. And then the child's heart bursts with a shout of joy or pain and immediately has a thousand echoes. But the child doesn't mean to give daily lessons in patriotism or of paternal and maternal love for children and even for his uncles and grandparents. Who does so makes the lively child a boring old man who finally wishes poetry didn't exist. Poetry, constrained to be social poetry, civil poetry, patriotic poetry, saddens his books, stales with the closed air of schoolrooms, and finally sickens with rhetoric, and dies. And we have had enough of this pseudo-poetry ever since Virgil died and Horace, growing old, closed the great revolution that began, one can say, and ended with the death of two women—Julia and Cleopatra—Caesar's daughter and his lover. Well, the crows—as Pindar would have called them—threw themselves cawing upon the immense battlefield, not to peck out the eyes of the dead, but the seed of poetry. And what did they do? They retold the history in those late poets, spicing things up with declamations, exclamations, curses; and they put it all in hexameters. But even they understood that verse alone doesn't make poetry; so they framed their versified history, threw in a description of dawn and another of dusk; and voilà there was a poem.[29]

Behold Giulio Montano, a poet like the others, inserting dawns and dusks at every opportunity, so that, grown tired of day-long recitations and unable to bear anymore, Natta Pinaro exclaimed, *"O I'll put up with him and listen one dawn to dusk!"* Good Natta didn't mean to be bored forever, and that after two or three verses he could go about his business.[30] It's pointless.

Horace already warned that delicate descriptions, smooth digressions, the beautiful rose, and yellow tropes weren't enough to turn prose into poetry.[31] For history to be poetry, it needs to filter through the marvel and innocence of our child soul, if we will still have one. We need to get distance on nearby facts, setting them at a remove from us.[32]

Do you want a way to distinguish poetry from pseudo-poetry in this kind of history?—If the versifier's narrative moves us less than the same historical facts in prose—you can simply say that the versifier has betrayed, has failed, has nothing of poetry. He has wasted his time and made us lose ours.

XII

But in Italy we want pseudo-poetry; we ask for it; we are enjoined to it. We Italians are victims of literary history! Truly, and not only in Italy, it seems to me that a false notion of letters has been generated. The humane letters are the instruments of ideas, ideas that order themselves into sciences. But fixated on the means, we have forgotten the ends. We're like farmers who only think about spades and talk about nothing but plows, and more about their beauty than their usefulness. We don't give a fig about seed, earth, and fertilizers. It therefore comes about that we have literati—physicists, philosophers, historians, mathematicians—like growers of hemp, grapes, grain, and olives, so to speak, so preoccupied with their spades and plows, that they don't bother with anything else and don't think they need to, and who feel that theirs is the most noble of occupations. At least the *farmers* made their own tools, but the literati "judge" those tools; they make "collections." This laziness governs our current criticism and literary history. Anyone can see that there are far more useful and better things to do: namely to cultivate and sow. But it is simply that among the many branches of literature, only poetry stands on its own, poetry contains everything in itself, all that one says and writes for his own or another's delight, love, bitterness, or sweetness. Poetry doesn't stand with respect to the sciences as the instrument stands to the end. It is cultivation, we submit, but of another order and species. It is, we submit, the entirely native cultivation of the primordial and perennial psyche. But we rank ourselves together with the "instrumental" literatures and talk in the same way. We divide things up by centuries and schools and call them Arcadian, Romantic, Classical, Realistic, Naturalistic, Idealistic, and so forth. We assert that literature progresses and decays, that it is born, dies, rises again, dies again. In truth poetry is such a marvelous thing that the true poetry you make now will be of the same quality as a true poetry of four thousand years ago.

How so? Thus: the human learns to speak so differently or so much better, year after year, century after century, millennium after millennium, but begins by suffering the same joys and sorrows in all times and places. The psychic substance is equal in the children of all people. A child is a child in the same way everywhere. And therefore: There's no such thing as Arcadian poetry, Romantic, Classical, Italian, Greek, or Sanskrit poetry, but only poetry, only poetry and . . . *not*-poetry.

Yes, there's counterfeit, sophisticated, imitation poetry, and it goes by many names. There are people who pipe like birds and seem to be birds when they whistle; but they aren't birds; they're bird-keepers. Now I can't say how pointless the story of these idlers is. Here it is in a few words: A poet emits a sweet song. For one century, or less, a thousand others repeat it, making it flowery and squandering it, to the point of boredom. And then another poet sings a sweet song, and for a century or more or less, another thousand work their variations on it. Sometimes the initial song is neither beautiful nor sweet, and what follows is even worse!

But in Italy and elsewhere, we aren't content to pay for this gathering. We have to overthink and make meaningless distinctions. That school was better, this one worse. We must return to that and repudiate this. No: Schools of poetry are always bad, and no one needs to join up. Poetry is poetry. For when one makes, for example, a real poem about a flock of sheep, and the readers later christen this true poet an Arcadian; and another gloriously magnifies some little thing in a real poem, and they proclaim him an embodiment of seventeenth-century excess, the critics are foolish and pedantic at the same time. The profound eyes of the interior child can contemplate anything, and the slightest thing can look huge.

You only have to judge (if you have this mania for judging) if those were eyes that *saw*. Set aside the "Seventeenth Century" and "Arcadia." Poetry doesn't evolve and involve, it is ever the light and fire, *that* light and *that* fire: These, when they appear, illuminate, and burn now as once upon a time, and in the same way.

One only has to add that it seldom appears. Yes, whether spoken or written, poetry is rare, pure poetry especially so. But there is *didactic* poetry, and didactic poetry includes great poems, great dramas, great romances. Now many imagine that all poetry is didactic, and this comprises a great sea. There are pearls in the sea, but how many? Very few; here more, and fewer there. One must also say that in these poems, dramas, romances, we seldom find pure poetry. Let me offer an example. One of these pearls, in the great pearly ocean is the *Divine Comedy*. Consider this field at evening:

> *Era già l'ora che volge il disio*
>   *ai naviganti, e intenerisce il core*
>   *lo dì ch'han detto ai dolci amici addio;*
> *e che lo nuovo peregrin d'amore*
>   *punge, se ode squilla di lontano*
>   *che paia il giorno pianger che si muore.*

> It was already that hour when longing
>   returns to sailors and softens the heart
>   of those who've said farewell to dear friends
> and the new pilgrim of love stings
>   if he hears the distances ring
>   as the dying day weeps.

One can't find a more poetic representation than this (Dante gives us the hour in which we become children again for a moment!), in which the most poetic touch is the last. It's the final but distant bell that weeps at the death of day, one of those effects that we versifiers have done to death. And so this bell can sound weak and dim to one gone deaf from all its duplications. But so it is. Well now, because of his art's demands, the poet had to put a bit of alloy into his pure gold.—What?—Why, the word "seems." He has to include it because he is describing another's poetic feeling, although he feels it too. And so he has said that the ringing *seems* to cry, not that it cries in reality. At one stroke (here a little and more elsewhere, most at others) the child on his way shakes himself and seems to be ashamed of being a child and of speaking in a childlike manner and corrects himself: *It seems* is not *we mean*. But dear child, we ourselves know that the bell doesn't cry, but only seems to cry, and also that the day seems to die but doesn't.[33]

XIII

That poetry which by its nature betters our love of country, family, and humanity is a blessing, a pure poetry which we rarely encounter. In Italy then, my own country (not yours, O Little One, you are the world's, not just for now but always), it is rarer than elsewhere. Indeed, we've never loved elemental and spontaneous poetry. As is generally so with our literature, our poetry specifically has always looked at models. Our style has been a reflection of Latin art, as the Latin was of Greek. This has endowed our writing with concreteness and majesty, but it has suffocated our poetry. Poetry isn't made from books. Then, too, we have loved ornament too much, and we especially put this taste on display where it least comports: in poetry.

The Italic Little One doesn't play unless well-dressed and groomed: The walnuts with which he plays his games must be gilded with gold and silver paper.[34] We always want honor: Always catching at the words of others and winking at our shadow, we look at ourselves instead of the playground. And we keep an eye on the public even more than at ourselves, casting sidelong glances at the great ones who stand around watching; and in this way we do everything without grace and agility. And since, in these times especially, everything's a contest or up for auction and always ends with adjudication and prize-giving, we want above all else to surpass one another and to win the judges' favor. The hocus-pocus of old men gets into our children's games, and jaded children come to prefer being first rather than being themselves. So our poetry (to call it such) is for the most part imitation, rather than harvest, and smells of lamp oil, not dew and fresh grass. We study too much to be poets, and it is superfluous to add that we study too little to know. We put study where it doesn't work.

But what's this—poetry doesn't have to do with study? Yes, but toward the end that Dante revealed. Virgil, who represents study, leads Dante to Matelda who embodies art; the arts in general and specifically—and Dante's art is specifically poetry. Thus study led Dante to poetry. And so with luminous eyes in the garden of innocence, Matelda, or poetry, gathers her flowers as she sings and purifies him in the river of forgetfulness and good will. This is to say that thanks to study, the poet has succeeded in recovering his childhood and just-so, sees well and selects without any weariness, and singing, chooses the flowers that appear at her feet.

Without insisting upon the moral value of such an exact and beautiful myth, and interpreting the poet in a poetic way, I would say that study must be directed more at removing than adding: at removing the rust of time from our soul, so that we can reflect upon the clarity of first things and dwell ourselves among them. Study must scour the impurities from the crystal found almost by chance, crystal that, even with its impurities, is worth more than a glass that we blow and shape while suffocating.

In short, study must make us innocent again, as Dante suggests when he places himself before Beatrice and Matelda: whereas Beatrice scolds him and makes him cry and shames him, a chastised child, he is like a baby before Matelda, who can't do things by himself and must be taken to be dipped in the water and to drink at the fountain. Our study must remove artifice and restore us to nature. So Dante says. His art is embodied in Matelda, who is human nature primordially free, happy, innocent.

XIV

But we Italians are, at bottom, too serious and clever to be poets. We imitate too much. And yes, through studying one must learn to do things differently, not the same way. But we want to do the same thing and believe or tell ourselves we're doing something better. Thus it often seems that setting another's jewel in our ring, we think we've found and even made the jewel ourselves; and more often, we imagine that gilding a bronze statue not only makes it more beautiful but makes it our own work. We no longer swing hammers at blocks of marble, we content ourselves with dusting and polishing beautiful statues. At the very most, we make the art of Giovanni Da Udine: elegant stuccos; but we don't remember that which he reportedly said to Pietro Aretino, who admired him: "They're big dolls!"[35]

And the schools knot us up, the schools are subtle iron wires, ever strung through the greenery of Matelda's forest: Gathering flowers, we fear tripping and falling at every step. I've already said it. If one abandons himself to the delights of the country, he fears being labeled Arcadian; if another sees an antithesis ahead of him, he equivocates, afraid of being called "seventeenth-century." Meanwhile the herd of imitators throws its bulk behind a larger ram, bleating or roaring after the fashion. Judging by those who write verses, one would think that at one moment the Italian only has a lover, and at the next only mamma. True poets are full of contradictory feelings; they don't want to be herded up under realism, idealism, or symbolism. Such concerns make them too cautious, too irresolute, too contrived. And Matelda withdraws, her sweet psalm drawing to an end, echoing ever more distantly, confounding the leaves with storm and stream with gurgling and death.

We lack—or seem to—a language for true and proper poetry.

Poetry emerges from the unnoticed particular, outside and within us.

Look at boys when they're seriously lost in play, and you'll see that they always have their hands on earthy things right in front of them—things that interest only them and that therefore only they see: snails, little bones, and little stones. The poet does the same. But what will we call these little ideal crystals, these stag beetles of his soul? The term hasn't been coined or divulged, or it isn't common to all nations or classes of people. Think of the flowers and birds that are the children's greatest and most familiar joy—what names do they have? Must one always just call them birds, regardless of whether they sing *how-ever* or *caw-caw*? Is it enough to say flowers or blooms, and to add, perhaps, vermilion and yellow, and not to draw distinctions between a hillside covered with marguerites and a field full of crocuses? Now if you insist on giving proper names here, the Linnaean binomial won't do, for a hundred reasons, and the common name varies, depending on the region, even from one region to another. If the Italian people paid attention to these flowers, plants, birds, insects, reptiles, that comprise in large part the poetry of the countryside, the names that they have in one place, would eventually prevail over others. But dazzled for the most part by the lightning flashes of Scipio's helmet, Italians aren't accustomed to chasing the subtler iridescence of dragonflies. And so the poet, if he wants to create, sometimes needs to let himself be told: *"And what is this? What does it mean? O poet, annoying know-it-all!"* Yet the poet has to go on, and let such things be said, hoping, if nothing else, that it will help future poets, who will recover such names formerly unknown and therefore called obscure. Truly, isn't he Adam who names things for the first time? So it must go, moment by moment, one renounces one's self-respect.

The art of the poet is always a renunciation. I've said one must take away, not add, and this is renunciation. One needs to scribble less about superficial beauties, pleasing to the eye, and gilded things connoting wealth: This is renunciation. Leave things raw and imperfect.—Oh, how necessary imperfection is to perfection! Martial also knew, who disparaged Maltho for wanting to call everything beautiful.[36] Tell us, he exclaimed, not just about the good, or the good and evil, but even just the evil! Continuous elegance is consummately sickly. It's like that luncheon in Morocco, described by De Amicis, where everything was covered with ointment.[37] Calling everything beautiful is totally anti-poetic; for poetry is artlessness; and that boy who does everything with a simpering and grimace, and always uses bloated, cloying words—what slaps to the back of the head that boy calls down, conscious of his childishness.

XV

With all this, what do you hope for? What's your goal? I return, you see, to my earlier point. To be useful to me? No, I've said. Useful to others? I said that, if so, it wasn't deliberate, and so isn't your goal. To delight yourself then? If this were your end, you would shut yourself up in our vision, and enjoy yourself and me, without those struggles that come with communicating the vision to others. Otherwise?...

Celebrity . . .

Oh poor boy!

Think, O Little One, how many other things you could do better suited to such an end. Leading an army or flying on a bicycle—just about anything else offers better prospects of glory. But let's suppose that you could get there "on the wings of song." What a disgrace it would be to put yourself on such a path, for you and me! First, it's time-consuming. Getting a big name requires mutual offices. I must converse, by letters and in person, consult with those who cultivate the same fields and get news about the efficacy of our manure, and exchange auguries and congratulations for a good harvest that we hope to have or have had. Yes, and also with those who profess only to furnish the seedlings, seed, chemical fertilizer, and tools, both manual and steam. How much study, how much diligence and patience one needs for such "cultivation." We need to gather up all our flowerpots, as peasants do, plant seeds and transplant many seedlings; we also pick up broken pots and the vases where the little peasant Ginevra's carnations grew. And always be on hand to water, prune, and to peek into the nearby jars and work at growing the biggest poppies and showiest sunflowers, and be ready to give and ward off the evil eye, and see things don't dry out.

But you will say: One has to get with the times! Well let me tell you something else. He doesn't reap who doesn't bend down to plant. Now in the interest of celebrity, one bends too far down, the seedlings are often so lowly, and one bends so often—there are so many. I mean to say that our soul (the *soul*, understand!) deforms itself, grows hunchbacked, like the poor peasants who bend to the grain. And you must be direct, serene, simple, of my soul!

Perhaps there isn't a sentiment in the world, not even the lust for gain that is so contrary to the innocence of the poet, as the chokehold of fame, which leads to a desire for domination. When you're infected by this disease, you (but this isn't about you) *I* don't look for the poetic, the good, and the beautiful, but for the sonorous and dazzling. Oh! at such times, I don't look for the minerals, jewels, the shells, the flowers before me, but wake anxiously, spying in notebooks of others, perhaps looking over the writer's shoulder at what he's putting down. Then I stop writing my verse and start doing as others: like today's tedious blackbird that doesn't sing his proper morning songs in the woods, but sounds the retreat. And why if not for desire for glory in his master and in him? Oh yellow-beaked blackbird you tried to be too clever! How can you believe that your *I see you!* that resounds among the falling dew, would be worse than that unbearable *Soldiers, pull back!?*

But truly *blackbird* means both sly and its opposite! O, and also we insist too much upon our own verse, or a single design, or habit, or genre that was once pleasing—and now the result is sickly—no, that's not enough—and we become false. We imitate ourselves, taking the glint of a water glass for the pure diamond we once found. Thinking or writing, an anxiety about effects always distracts us—*What will we say here? Will this or something else impress them?* And your grace, which isn't grace if it isn't spontaneous, is lost forever. You don't see more justly and clearly; indeed you don't see at all anymore, and worst of all, as I said, you don't see how you change your clothes and even your soul with others you think are worth more than you!

XVI

Don't think about celebrity, Little One: it isn't for you. It's either too difficult or easy to come by. Difficult: Haven't I already said how seldom they understand you? You don't do anything but discover the new in the old; the others—your readers and listeners—think or say nothing but, *How true it is! And I hadn't thought of it*—but you hardly ever receive such blessings. Today people stare at their navels so fixedly that they can't see or talk about anything else. And because the stupor of their egoism has covered the light, they say that you're obscure. You can describe a country morning as fully as you want, for example, but one who hasn't even seen the sun rise in the city, much less the country, can't understand or value anything you say.

Furthermore, you are often obscure for another reason: because you're clear. Readers today are habituated to pinwheels, whirligigs, tangles of thought and sentiment; because the authors, drawing from this and that in their books, lay stucco and gold leaf over the works to make them look new, or act like hares running in circles and hopping around in order to hide their tracks from hunters. Readers have grown so accustomed to mysteries and hocus-pocus from writers grown too comfortable, always trying to outsmart you, that when you say something simple about simple things, no one understands you anymore.

They're looking for something in you that isn't there, and because they don't find it, they treat us badly. And even if they understand you, it means they understand only that you don't want to say other than what you say, and imply nothing, and you don't offer the absurd and common pretence that the meaning of your work is what the readers put there, and so they value you all the less. For most people it seems the beautiful resides in ornamental friezes and the poetic in rhetorical fevers. How can anyone ever hear the storming of leaves, the rush of a stream, or the song of your oaten flute as you want, when the village band deafens the countryside with trombones and the beating of a bass drum?

No, no, Little One, fame or celebrity derive from the approval of many, and only a few hear, listen, and approve of you. It's true that you call on all, but remember: not to the men but the children like you inside them. Now although no one is missing an inner child, few will give you an ear. And do you know who these few are? For the most part, poets. That is, their inner child, and he's listening only because he sings, too, and wants to know if you sing better or worse, or he's standing by, waiting for you to finish singing.

And what happens? It happens that one day or another he begins to make your verse. First he just picks up a few notes, then your rhythm and finally your whole song. And then? Then he becomes your imitator. Well?—Well, the imitator is a debtor and the debtor sooner or later comes to speak ill of his creditor, and so, also among these few, many steal from your praises in order to assure their own. And your fame either isn't born or expires promptly on birth.

XVII

But would you feel like accepting that kind of renown? You know where celebrity comes from. Generally, it derives from self-promotion, as our Leopardi put it so well: "The most direct way to acquire fame is by asserting firmly, and with pertinacity, in as many ways possible that one already has it."[38] And elsewhere: "In general, in our century that esteemed person is rare, whose honors didn't originate in his own mouth . . . Who wants to elevate himself— however much true virtue might be there—sends modesty packing."[39] And you, my boy, would you have me climb on a chair or a stage to sing your praises or shout your fame? "*This boy is a* Wunderkind, *noted throughout the world . . .*" Such facile celebrity! But you, no, you wouldn't want that. Well, people will never believe someone's really important if that importance doesn't overwhelm whatever modesty he might possess. If your modesty is great, content yourself with a very modest greatness. You will be seen as a mediocre poet and since a poet can't be a mediocrity, they will judge you not to be a poet.

Or will you, not giving credence to Leopardi's bitter thoughts, expect your praises to originate in the mouths of others? To confer true fame, such praises would have to spread among a great number of people, who would praise without knowing you, not having heard you, not having read you! They will praise you by hypnotic suggestion. Oh! The worst thing that could happen to you! They'll praise everything you've done equally: That which you feel to be the best would be placed beside that which you know to be your worst. Even things that you haven't written but which appear under your name would be praised to the stars, and so preferred above things which you have written and think good and beautiful! And what would you do with such celebrity?

All the more reason you need to see the source of those first praises that produced all the others. From what? From something more apt than anything else to blind and intoxicate people, to make them delirious. From politics, for example, from party or from sect. Watch out, my boy. It's the case that anyone who wants to grab celebrity has to tap that barrel where everyone drinks. The great barrel is politics, the wine that everyone drinks is personal feeling—the communal barrel warms us up—your renown is common drunkenness!

O illustriousness unworthy of your desire. And bitter afterwards. You know that we live in a competitive time and age of sorting and award-giving. People's greatest entertainment is judging others. In ancient times, Athens had a similar competitive mania about drawing lots that determined seating at the great court of Heliaia (ʽΗλιαια).[40] Today there's not just that insanity, but many; and they don't just judge, for want of other things, dogs and house-cats, but domestic and foreign writers and poets. They judge and they classify: This one comes first, this one second, third, and so on. Oh, and you, Little One, make your little discourse, express a feeling, expound a thought, smile, shed a tear, without looking at yourself, without knowing it, one can say, without reason, to the first stranger, venting your heart, almost outside yourself— through your words, your laugh, your tears, and here you feel that your auditor catches it, weighs your phrases, sketches your smile in the air with his thumb, examines the water and the crystal of your tears, and whispers, "Not bad! Pretty good! Good! Wonderful! There are certainly worse. Even better than others! First! Second! Third! Major poet! Minor poet!"

Surely you—if you're not incredibly vain or a sniveller—wipe the smile off your face, drink back your tears, and so forth. Maybe you decide in that moment not to go further than others and to enjoy life or cry to yourself once more. But you're a child and you always return to the beginning, only to see every time that there's no room for children in this world! The fact is that beyond the tedium of always feeling judged, as if you were a scholastic exercise, you can also taste the bitterness of being put off by a quick or nasty judgement and also of being put at the head of those you never dreamed of emulating, never thought of, would never, could never think of, engrossed as you were in your pleasure or pain. They compare you to others and also to yourself. They count your years, your crow's feet, and your white hairs and can't wait to tell you your time has passed the hour of reckoning, that you're wasted, an imbecile, dying. Beautiful charity! And one fine day, they will throw you into a song, forgetting you, and wrongly. Always wrongly because the good work you did must not be negated by the inferior that followed; and because such a prodigy can never be born to make one forget that before him they found hardly a trace of poetry. Great as it would be if they added the poet to the canon, he can only sit on one chair, or let us say a throne: He doesn't need two, or all of them; and that another poet or all of them get up and go off.

Cheap fame isn't for you my child. Reading the purest poetry makes the vulgar say: *How much better it could be done, and then some!*

Truly this is the illusion of an ornamentalist . . . And I think of gingerbreads decorated with flowers of sugar, so pretty, that people look at them so longingly, only to throw away the decorated one and eat the plain thing.

But also let this childish example of decorated gingerbread remind you that generally one admires and praises what's above, not what is below. Remember that true poetry inspires the heart to beat, rather than the hands to clap.

XVIII

So . . . But I get it: You do not aspire to celebrity but immortality, and so you distinguish between celebrity among the living and fame after death. I don't want to tell you (your illusions are dear to me); I don't want to tell you that we won't hear anything they say about us. I will hear or at least you will hear: Don't be glum. But will you hear beautiful things? Here's the point.

And above all: Will they say nothing about us? We race through our lives these days, and visits to the graveyard are a waste of time. Life today makes us deaf to the faint screeching of shadows. The dead don't count any more now. A poet said that the day of death is the day of praise, but that doesn't hold after a few years. Giovanni Prati himself knows what the grave holds![41] And this oblivion that presses immediately upon the dead, however literary, is not without reason or justice. We literati want to take up too much of the world around us. If we stayed in our corner, if we didn't throw our arms open so much among others, if we stayed so loud, we would have this compensation of silence after death. Now, will they say nothing about you? And if they do, will it be good and just? Do you really believe that the mania of grading, the artificial awe, the blindness of parties and sects will come to an end then?

Look: Often the dead are troubled in their repose and dragged out to be used by the living. Very often. You know the forms in which envy so often expresses itself. You give one his due praise in the presence of someone. They briefly confirm this: Then from far away one turns to praise another, who can be inferior or superior to the one you praised, but is almost always dead. Now you, my boy, would be exhumed to this end? As a shade, will you have the pleasure of shading a good solid boy, who lives and sings? You wouldn't like this: better to sleep forgotten. It's better just to be dead than to continue to appear before tribunals to be judged and classified, since what the judges pass down and is fixed forever is the light of their torches.

You don't want judgments: You want to move, you want assent, love, and not for you but for your poetry. Well, when you're dead, if your voice was pure, if it was the voice of the soul and of things, not the echo, whether dim or strong, of another voice; well that voice would go unremarked upon, where it is not forgotten. In truth, and reasonably so, though often repeated, it will founder in time, I can't say whether in silence or in the surrounding sound: like the chirping of swallows under your gutters, a piece that you hear and then don't hear any longer . . .

You want to speak? Wait: I haven't finished.

In any case how should it be otherwise? What do you really do that's worthy of praise and glory? You laugh, you cry — what merit in that? If you believe you have worth, it's a sign that you laugh and cry on purpose; if you do it on purpose, it's not your poetry; if it isn't your poetry, you're not worthy of praise. You discover — it is said — you don't contrive; and that which you discover was there before you and will go on without you. Would you write down your name? You get angry because they want to judge and also give you a prize for that which is just your nature and your manifestation of life. What then does your name matter?

XIX

O LITTLE ONE

The name? The name?
I sow the soul,
that white thing at the core,
    that's lost on earth
        but gives birth to the beautiful green tree.

I don't want laurel or bronze, but to live,
and life is blood, a river that rises and falls
    no louder than
        the faintest pulse.

I want my heartbeat to stay in your hearts
with no more pride than a breeze,
    trembling on water, troubles the stone
        that rests in the depths.

I want to plant a single sigh in the air
I want to be the wailing owl
    among river willows,
        I too, in the dark, I too.

If bells cry and cry
in the invisible opacity of evenings
    I want to be near
        the one that cries, to that breath.

I want little — just to add one point
to the Milky Way's worlds,
    in infinite sky:
        to give new sweetness to the primal cry.

I want to leave my life
hanging from every stem, on every petal,
    a dew exhaled from sleep
        to fall in our brief dawn.

With the rainbow's thousand droplets
that sublime themselves in the single sun
    and come to nothing,
        leaving more life than before.

XX

Good! I'll summarize then, like the serious man I am. Poetry which is poetry
in itself, without being "moral," "civic," "patriotic," or "social" poetry, is good
for morality, civil society, country, and society. The poet must not have,
does not have another end (I'm not speaking about riches, celebrity, or fame)
than that of merging with nature, where he leaves an accent, ray, palpitation,
new and eternal—his own. Poets have brightened the eyes, memory, human
thought, earth, the sea, sky, love, pain, virtue, and people who haven't heard
their name; for the names people say and value are always or almost always
followers, ingenious copiers, elegant bowdlerizers, if they aren't meaningless
names. When true poetry flowered—that, I mean, that which one finds
instead of making, discovers instead of contriving—one paid attention to the
poem, not the poet, whether he was old or young, good looking or ugly, bald
or with long hair, fat or thin, where he was born, how he grew up, when he
died. Such trivialities lead to legend-making, critical studies, interrogations,
when the poet wants to call attention and admiration only to the poetry. And
it was bad. And it's forever getting worse—the poets of our time search out
only the vanity of personality rather than the jewels I have described.

   Not those first ones. And you, my boy, would make that which the first ones
made, with the reward that they received, the recompense you deem great: For
though unnamed, true poets live in the things which they made for us.

   Is it so?

Yes.

Endnotes

NOTE TO THE READER

The textual apparatus includes notes by both Pascoli and myself. To distinguish between them, each is prefaced by either [Pascoli] or [Translator]. As it is useful to see Pascoli's frequent references to Virgil, Horace, and other writers in context, I have included English translations for his citations, relying on H. Rushton Fairclough's versions for Virgil and Horace. On five occasions where no further comment is needed, these citations are preceded by [Fairclough].

1. [Pascoli] Plato, Phaedrus, 77E. And Cebes with a smile, "How we were afraid," he said, "O Socrates, show us, or better, persuade us not to be fearful, but perhaps there is also a little child in us who is afraid of such things: let us try, too, not to fear death like birdlime."

2. [Pascoli] Homer doesn't expressly say that Phemius is old, but he does so indirectly with the epithet *periclytos* (*Odyssey* 1, 325), as with the other bard, Demodicus (ibid., 8, 521 et al.) and specially with that which Phemius affirms of himself (ibidem 22, 347):

> *I am my own teacher, as a god planted in my heart*
> *Every reason of song ...*

Which is consonant with Penelope's words (ibidem 1, 337 ff.):

Phemius, you who know many other evils of people
Works of men and gods ...

And the old Phemius with a song newer or younger (ibidem, 351 ff.):

> *Poi che gli uomini pregiano ed amano piú quel canto*
> *che il piú nuovo all'intorno de li ascontanti riuoni.*

How much the ancient and truthful Väinämöinen, I remember from that marvelous fragment of the version of P.E. Pavolini (*Sul limitare,* pp. 75 ff.):

The *ancient* and truthful Väinämöinen

Thus the *ancient* Väinämöinen

When they heard the new song
they felt its sweet sound.

[Translator] Väinämöinen, who might seem out-of-place in a work that otherwise
leans on Greek and Roman sources (not to mention Indo-European), is a protagonist
of the Finnish *Kalevala*. Such is an indication of Pascoli's breadth of study. Paolo Emilio
Pavolini was a prolific and wide-ranging translator of Buddhist texts, Tennyson, and *A
Thousand and One Nights* into Italian.

3. [Pascoli] Homer, Odyssey, 8.499; *phaîne d'aoidén*. Note that I'm not asserting
the etymology of *aeidein* from *a-* not and *vid-* to see [vedere]. No, I mean that the
ancient singer was aware of the connection. Two verses from the Odyssey should be
compared, 1.337 ff., the first of which ends with *oîdas* and the second with *aoidoí*.
One reflects on 8.64: Eyes are absent, but he gives us the sweet *aoidén*. I even dare
to say, one finds it useful to observe, concerning the blinding of Polyphemus the
cannibal and drunkard that Polyphemus beyond being the name of the terrible
Cyclops is an epthet of the *aoidós* Phemius (22.376), Phemius, whose name resembles
the second-half of Polyphemus's. And the cyclops shows his musicality in the
Odyssey only when (9.315):

> With his flageolet he parried the sheep to the mountain

After all, this musicality is in his name, if this counts, as in 2.150, "full of whispers or
voices." In Theocritus the Cyclops is a sweet singer of love, and no one among the
others knows how to play the flute as well as he (Theocritus, *Idylls* 11).

[Translator] Polyphemus is the subject of Theocritus *Idylls* 6 and 11. Luckless in his love
for Galatea, he laments his ugliness.

4. [Pascoli] I remember that we were all to believe that the *Divine Comedy* was begun
in the poet's forty-eighth year, or later. And that it is a poem of contemplation rather
than of the active life.

5. [Pascoli] Thus Mazzoni truly represented the Muses (one was enough) that
accompanied "the bad faith represented with the right vowels."

6. [Pascoli] It's not modern poets alone, so absolutely fixated on love and woman, but
the ancient tragic poets as well, and even the choral poet who immediately followed
the epic poetry, who gave a feminine and erotic coloring to the Homeric poems.
And the women mentioned in those poems weren't enough, and so new ones were
created. This increased the dramatic interest of the cycle, but diminished their poetic
essence. Thus *Orlando Innamorato* and *Furioso* with their love are more dramatic but
less poetic than Roland in the *Song*.

7. [Pascoli] Augusto Conti tells us of a girl: *When she saw the moon or the stars she cried out in joyous voices, and pointed them out to me, and called to them like living things, offering them whatever she had at hand, even her clothes.* When I pass again in thought to all the poems that I have read, I find no greater poetry than here.

8. [Pascoli] This for example is what Andromache says as she weeps over Hector (II.22,510):

> *Nudo, e sì che di vesti ce n'hai ne la casa riposte,*
> *Morbide e graziose, lavoro di mani di donne!*

9. [Translator] *Nepenthe* and *ácholon:* mythological drugs, the former of forgetfulness, a remedy for sorrow, and the latter for anger.

10. [Translator] isosyllabics — a verse form in which all syllables are of the same length; homeoteleuton — the repetition of like endings, near-rhyme.

11. [Pascoli] Plato, *Phaedrus,* III B.

12. [Translator] *Parthenias,* "virgin," is a common epithet of Athena, but here Pascoli is thinking of Virgil, to whom it was also applied.

13. [Pascoli] Cato, *Agricoltura* 2.7. *Armenta delicula, oves deliculas.* I translate thus, departing from Keil. Cfr. for the meaning of *armenta,* Virgil, *Georgics* 3.129.

14. [Pascoli] Varro, *Rerum Rusticarum* 1.17.
[Translator] Belvoir's 1918 version of the passage.

> I have spoken of the four points of husbandry which relate to the land to be cultivated and also of those other four points which have to do with the outside relations of that land: now I will speak of those things which pertain to the cultivation of the land. Some divide this subject into two parts, men and those assistants to men without which agriculture cannot be carried on. Others divide it into three parts, the instruments of agriculture which are articulate, inarticulate and mute: the articulate being the servants, [73] the inarticulate the draught animals, and the mute being the wagons and other such implements.

F. H. Belvoir, *Roman Farm Management: The Treatises of Cato and Varro Done Into English, With Notes of Modern Instances* (New York: The Macmillan Company, 1913), 106.

15. [Pascoli] Virgil 3.126 ff.
[Translator] Fairclough's version.

> "They cut him flowering grasses, and give fresh water and corn, that he may be more than equal to the seductive toil, and no feeble offspring may repeat the

leanness of the sires. But the mares themselves they purposely make spare, and when now the familiar pleasure first prompts them to union, they withhold leafy fodder and debar them from the springs.

Virgil: Eclogues, Georgics, Aeneid 1-6, trans. H. R. Fairclough, rev. G. P. Goold (Cambridge: Harvard University Press, 1999), 185, 187.

16. [Pascoli] Virgil, ibidem, 174 ff.
[Fairclough] "Meanwhile you will not feed their unbroken youth on grass alone or poor willow leaves and marshy sedge, but on young corn, plucked by hand." (Fairclough, *Virgil*, 189).

17. [Pascoli] Cato, *Agricoltura* 58, and read 56 and 59.
[Translator] For the relevant chapters, see Belvoir, as above, 167-170.

18. [Pascoli] Virgil, *Aeneid* 5.284; Pholoë, a Cretan woman expert in weaving, with twins at the breast, is given as a prize to Sergestus. This is an imitation of Homer, *Iliad* 23.263. We also find *serva* [slave] at 9.546. Licinna who gives a son, Elenore, to the king of the Lydians. And this, too, is in Homer. Furthermore, Andromache gives birth in servitude: *Aeneid* 3.327 and there is the idea and word *servitude* with regard to bulls in the *Georgics* 3.168, and the same, that is of Tityrus, in the *Eclogues* 1.41.
[Translator] The relevant passages from Fairclough's *Virgil: Aeneid,* Book V. "Aeneas presents Sergestus with his promised reward, glad that the ship is saved and the crew brought back. A slave woman is given him, skilled in Minerva's tasks, Pholoë, of Cretan stock, with twin boys at her breast" (Fairclough, *Virgil*, 491).

Aeneid, Book III "We . . . have endured the pride of Achilles' son and his youthful insolence, bearing children in slavery" (Ibid., 393, 395).

In the *Georgics*, as Fairclough notes, the "free necks" of oxen are yoked with collars rather than yokes. "Then when their free necks are used to servitude, yoke the bullocks in pairs linked from the collars themselves, and force them to step together" (Ibid., 189).

And from the *Eclogues,* Eclogue I. "What was I to do? I could not quit my slavery nor elsewhere find my gods so ready to aid. Here, Meliboeus, I saw that youth for whom our altars smoke twice six days a year. Here he was the first to give my plea an answer: 'Feed, swains, your oxen as of old; rear your bulls'" (Ibid., 27, 29).

19. [Pascoli] Virgil, *Aeneid* 1.701, ff. 705; 5.391; 8.411, 584.

20. [Pascoli] Virgil, *Eclogues* 1.28.
[Fairclough] "Freedom, who though late, yet cast her eyes upon me in my sloth, when my beard began to whiten as it fell beneath the scissors" (Fairclough, *Virgil,* 27).

21. [Pascoli] Varro, *Rerum Rusticarum*, 1.17: *ipsi colunt, ut perique pauperculi cum sua progenie.*
[Translator] "They till, as the poor do, with their families."

22. [Pascoli] *Georgics* 2.458 ff.; 1.300 ff. and elsewhere.

23. [Pascoli] *Virgil*, ibidem, 4.125 ff. [Translator] This is Virgil's famous discussion of beekeeping

24. [Pascoli] Virgil, *Georgics* 2.458 ff.; 1.300 ff. and elsewhere.
[Fairclough] "O happy husbandmen! Too happy should they come to know their blessings, for whom, far from the clash of arms, most righteous Earth, unbidden, pours forth from her soil an easy sustenance. What though no stately mansion with proud portals disgorge at dawn from all its halls a tide of visitors" (Fairclough, *Virgil*, 169).

And then:

"Winter is the farmer's lazy time. In cold weather farmers chiefly enjoy their grains, and feast together in merry companies" (Ibid., 121).

25. [Pascoli] Horace, Sermons 2.6, 1 ff.
[Fairclough] "This is what I prayed for! A piece of land not so very large, where there would be a garden, and near the house a spring of ever-flowing water, and up above these a bit of woodland. More and better than this have the gods done for me. I am content." *Horace: Satires, Epistles, Ars Poetica*, trans. H. R. Fairclough, (Cambridge: Harvard University Press, 1942), 210–11.

26. [Translator] This may be the essay's richest allusion. Pascoli is pointing to a passage in *Purgatorio xxii* (67 ff.) in which the Latin poet Statius praises Virgil for carrying a torch behind him in order to illumine the road for those who followed. Statius goes on to celebrate Virgil's *Eclogue IV,* prophecy of the birth of a child who will usher in a new age of justice and harmony, lines which Christian readers long took as a reference to the birth of Christ. Pascoli, though, has a different little one in mind!

27. [Pascoli] Plato, *The Apology* 28B. ff.; Virgil, *Georgics* I.291 ff.

28. [Pascoli] Virgil, *Aeneid* 8.155 ff.
[Translator] Evander greets Aeneas, whose coming has been foretold, and welcomes him with a feast.

29. [Pascoli] Seneca, *Epistles* II.122: cfr: *Apoc. 2*
[Translator] Epistle 122, *On Darkness as a Veil for Wickedness*, satirizes the corruption of Nero's Rome, the youth of which have inverted the natural order of things, drinking before eating, eating before swimming, making night day and day night. This inversion of the natural order is a recurrent theme in Pascoli as noted in the introduction, above:

> Le rondini viaggiatrici insegnarono all'uomo di fermarsi. E gli dettero il modellino della casa. Solo, l'uomo lo capovolse.

"And they gave people a little model for the house. Only, man turned it upside-down."

30. [Pascoli] Seneca, *Epistles* II.122. And continue, reading the anecdote which follows: "Febo went to take the burning lamp outside, and the rosy day began to spread its light on earth; and already the sad sparrow assiduously began to bring food to the chattering nest, and to feed it, well-divided with its moist beak, and thus Varus exclaimed, 'It's the hour that Buta goes to bed.' Because Buta was an avoider of light, an insomniac, who made night day. A little later, Montano declaimed, 'already the shepherds retrieve their tools from the hut; already night begins to bring dark silence to the lulled earth.' And Varus: 'what are you saying? It's already night. I'm going to offer my morning greeting to Buta.'"

31. [Pascoli] Horace, *The Art of Poetry* 15 ff.
[Translator] This is part of Horace's opening indictment of poetic excess. Fairclough translates:
Works with noble beginnings and grand promises often have one or two purple patches so stitched on
as to glitter far and wide, when Diana's grove and altar, and

The winding stream a-speeding 'mid fair fields

or the river Rhine, or the rainbow is being described.
For such things there is a place, but not just now. (Fairclough, Horace, 451).

32. [Pascoli] Do you have binoculars? Set them toward the country, toward a house, toward a village. Look through in the usual way, behold prose. Turn them around: there is poetry. More particulars in the first and more distinct. More vision in the second and more ... poetry. Try it!

33. [Pascoli] It's superfluous to note that for all that isn't poetry in Dante's *Comedy* (and not all the poetry that is there is pure), the poem is in its general conception the most poetic poem there is and will be in the world. Nothing is more appropriate to the soul's childhood than the contemplation of the invisible, the pilgrimage though mystery, conversation, weeping, humility and enjoyment taken among the dead.

34. [Translator] As RosaMaria LaValva points out on page 53 of *The Eternal Child: The Poetry and Poetics of Giovanni Pascoli* (Chapel Hill, N.C., 1999), Pascoli is thinking specifically of *filetto*, a board game resembling checkers or tic-tac-toe.

35. [Translator] Da Udine: Giovanni Nanni, also Giovanni de' Ricamatori, better known as Giovanni da Udine (1487–1564). Vasari discusses the uncanny realism of the artist's stucco creations at the beginning of volume five of his Lives. Aretino records Giovanni da Undine's comment about dolls in a letter to Lodovico Dolce, dated June 25, 1537. See: *Il primo libro delle lettere di Pietro Aretino* (Milan: G. Daelli, 1864), 184.

36. [Translator] Pascoli refers to Martial, *Epigrams* X.46:
"You want all you say to be smart, Maltho. Say sometimes what also is good; say what is middling; say sometimes what is bad." (Walter C. A. Ker M. A., trans., *Martial: Epigrams II,* Book X, XLVI (New York: G.P. Putnam's Sons, 1919), 189.

37. [Translator] Edmondo De Amicis:
> I understood in one moment how it was that a people who ate in that way should believe in another God, and take other views of human life than ours. I cannot express what I felt otherwise than by likening myself to some unhappy wretch who is forced to satisfy his appetite upon the pomatum pots of his barber. There were flavours of soaps, pomades, wax, dyes, cosmetics—everything that is least proper to be put in a human mouth. At each dish we exchanged glances of wonder and dismay. No doubt the original material was good enough— chickens, mutton, game, fish; large dishes of a very fine appearance, but all swimming in most abominable sauces, and so flavoured and perfumed that it would have seemed more natural to attack them with a comb rather than with a fork. (Edmondo De Amicis, *Morocco: Its People and Places*, C Rollin-Tilton, trans. (London, 1882), 46.

38. [Translator] This is Leopardi's *"Pensiero* LX."

> *Dice il La Bruyère una cosa verissima, che è più facile ad un libro mediocre di acquistar grido per virtù di una riputazione già ottenuta dall'autore, che ad un autore di venire in riputazione per mezzo di un libro eccellente. A questo si può soggiungere, che la via forse più diritta di acquistar fama, è di affermare con sicurezza e pertinacia, e in quanti più modi è possibile, di averla acquistata.*

> Bruyère says something very true: that it's easier for a mediocre book to gain renown by virtue of a reputation the author already has, than for an author to gain a reputation for an excellent book. To this one can add, that possibly the most direct way to getting famous is by affirming with one certainty and persistence, and in as many ways as possible, of already having it.

39. Leopardi, *Pensiero* 24.

O io m'inganno, o rara è nel nostro secolo quella persona lodata generalmente, le cui lodi non sieno cominciate dalla sua propria bocca. Tanto è l'egoismo, e tanta l'invidia e l'odio che gli uomini portano gli uni agli altri, che volendo acquistar nome, non basta far cose lodevoli, ma bisogna lodarle, o trovare, che torna lo stesso, alcuno che in tua vece le predichi e le magnifichi di continuo, intonandole con gran voce negli orecchi del pubblico, per costringere le persone sì mediante l'esempio, e sì coll'ardire e colla perseveranza, a ripetere parte di quelle lodi. . . .Chi vuole innalzarsi, quantunque per virtù vera, dia bando alla modestia. Ancora in questa parte il mondo è simile alle donne: con verecondia e con riserbo da lui non si ottiene nulla.

I either deceive myself, or in our century it's rare that a person is widely praised, whose praises don't begin in his own mouth. The egotism is such, and envy and the hatred men bear one again the others, who want to get a name for themselves. It's not enough to do praiseworthy things, but one needs to be praised or to find, looking around oneself, someone who can praise in his place and glorify him continuously, ringing out grandly in the ears of the public, to force people to see his example, and with ardor and perseverance to repeat his praises. . . . Who wants to put himself out there, however real his virtue may be, has to abandon modesty. In this regard the world still resembles womankind: one doesn't get anywhere with modesty and reserve.

40. [Translator] *Heliastae* or jurors date from Solon.

41. [Translator] Giovanni Prati (1815-1884), Italian romantic poet. Pascoli's reference in his previous sentence "day of praise" (dal dì della lode), i.e., the day of one's death, alludes to Prati's Canto:

Dio ti guardi dal dì della lode,
Che ogni labro, ogni cor ti rammenti!

May God look out for you on the day of praise,
When every lip, every heart remembers you!

See Ginevra Bastianelli, *Album Di Omaggio Letterario ad Alessandro Manzoni* (Rome: Tipografia Bencini, 1874), 91.

III. POEMS

A NOTE ON THE TRANSLATION

I have translated Pascoli's poems, with their intricate rhymed music, into unrhymed verse rather than sacrifice meaning for the sake of a "jingling sound of like endings" in contemporary American English. Still the reader should know that on the other side of the translation's veil we have sestina rhyme-schemes (*Fog*), the *rispetto toscano* (a form of popular song derived from the Sicilian *strambotto* and dating from the origins of Italian literature [*Fides*]), sonnet (*The Nest*), and sundry variations on the ballad and *ballata piccola*. Many of the poems from *Myricae* translated here are a traditional Italian poem of ten lines, divided into two tercets and a final quatrain (cf. Hopkins's "curtal" sonnet).

Similarly, it is difficult to convey in such a short selection the importance which the poetic sequence had for Pascoli. By the end of the nineteenth century, such groupings of poems had become familiar through the influence of Baudelaire, although for Italian poets the history reaches back beyond Petrarch and Dante. A comparison of Pascoli editions shows that he was constantly reordering his poems, in search of a best and most natural order. He was keenly aware of how the juxtaposing of two poems can create additional thematic or emotional values. Sometimes the connections between poems can even be syntactic, as when the pupil of an eye at the end of *A Black Cat* is discovered to be open in the following poem, *And Then?* Similarly, the ticking with which *And Then?* ends anticipates the sound of the following poem.

Pascoli was at once poet, scholar, and naturalist. Homer, Virgil, and Dante are often present in subtle ways, and Mazzoni's *I promessi sposi* haunts the background of many poems, especially those that touch on domestic life. He also has the intimate knowledge of the botanical world that one would expect of a naturalist, and this makes its demands both on the translator and reader. Gianfranca Lavezzi's edition of *Myricae* not only glosses Pascoli's myriad classical sources but also includes a botanical atlas. For all these reasons, I have chosen poems that will be accessible to the contemporary reader, trusting that some will choose to look deeper into Pascoli's world.

from **THE TAMARISKS**

Myricae (1886–1894)

TUMULT

Scalpitio

You hear the galloping
(Are you afraid? ...)
Speeding across the plains to you,
shuddering fast.

An infinite, bare plain:
unbroken, vast, empty, flat
— that fissure
a lost bird's shadow —

Nothing else.
Fleeing
remote disaster,
where and what no one knows
on heaven and earth.

You hear the galloping —
Stronger, pounding
across the plains for you —
Death! Death! Death!

CRUST

Il rosicchiolo

She saved it just for you,
just you, poor angel — here —
O, such weeping!
See? It's a crust of dry bread.

She died on a straw pallet;
you slept safely, poor angel.
Such weeping! What hunger!
But there was a crust of hard bread.

She waked those long hours,
wept over you and died of weeping,
hunger and love,
and look! Here's a crust of bread.

THEN

Allora

Then that time so long
ago — happy — very — not now
but that sweetness
that sweetness then!

That year! and years fled
and fly and will —
You can't — don't think it —
ever again!

A day like no other
doesn't return.
It's a phantasm
before and after.

One point! in no time
forever gone really so
beautiful — I was
so happy once happy.

HOMELAND

Patria

What trembling —
cicadas
whirring shrilly,
the Mistral stirring
crumpled leaves,

shafts of dusty
sunset through elms:
two lonely clouds,
rusty, two white
brush strokes

in such deep blue.

Pomegranate hedge,
tamarisk thicket,
a distant thresher
throbbing
the silver angelus . . .

Where was I? The bells
told me where.
Weeping while a dog
barked at this foreigner
who walked with bent head.

DEATH AND SUN

Morte e sole

Study death: a mournful
constellation glinting in black sky,
short word, bright vision
   read, o pupil —

You can't. Thus the fixed
star burns in solitary heaven.
If you look at the sun, eye, what do you see?
   empty whirling, a nothing.

THE PAST

Il passato

I return to the places where I wept.
The weeping face is smiling now —
I return to the places where I smiled —
O that smile full of tears!

FIDES

When dusk burns its coppery light
and the cypress turns gold, pure gold,
Mother tells her little one
how it's a garden up there.

And the sleeping boy dreams
golden branches, golden trees, a forest of gold,
while flayed by night's black wind
a cypress weeps in the storm.

DEAD

Morto

What've you got there, little hand
shut in the great sleep — what've you got?
Tell me? Oh, it's pointless —
no one will ever know what you hold.

The Angel brought you a gift
while you slept; hold it tight forever.
It was night; there was no morning.
It's yours now, child, so sleep.

ORPHAN

Orfano

The snow falls softly, softly falls:
Listen: a wicker cradle rocks slowly, slowly.
The infant cries, finger in mouth.
The old woman sings, her chin on her hand.

The old woman sings: Roses and lilies
surround your bed — a beautiful garden.
Baby's asleep in that beautiful garden.
The snow falls softly, softly falls.

ABANDONED

Abbandonato

Alone in the attic, naked, dying,
his weeping fills the rafters like bird song.

The Saint tells him — a little longer; take heart —
He murmurs — I've waited so long for bread —

The Angel says — The Savior's coming —
He sighs — just give me a blanket —

The Virgin speaks — Your pain is over! —
— O I want mamma, and to sleep at her breast —

The storm weeps drop by drop
into the attic. The Saint watches, seated;

The angel looks on, pale as wax.
The Virgin weeps through her smile.

The child falls silent, waits till dusk,
big eyes on the door, watching, fixed.

Night falls. Shadows deepen;
He's off to Paradise all by himself.

THE OWL

La civetta

They were black in the moonlight,
sheer cypresses, basalt spires,
when a shadow unfurled swiftly
      from the shadows above,

a dream trace of feathered flight,
a trace of velvet-soft breath
that left the shadows and slipped
      through the pale and silent light;

and the cypresses on the empty shore
were a columned blackness,
rigid, each holding a nest
      fallen asleep in its branches.

And above such life asleep
in the cypresses, in the center of the heath,
sounds — listen — the shrill laugh
      of a witch

and perhaps a shrill threat
overwhelms the brief, timid
chirpings of all that life
      throbbing in cypresses.

Through the sky's depths, death passes
with wings gentle as breath,
with open eyes above the sad,
          sleeping world.

Death, the sharp blast of your singular
laughter moves the shadow that silently
covers us, and suddenly awakens
          wailing; cringing

and when all seems asleep
in those trees, every life still trembling
in its nest, the air is
          scarred with your cry.

THE HUNTER

Il cacciatore

Suddenly: An idea spins in motionless air!
She sings in the sky. The hunter sees,
hears, follows: His heart swims inside.

If then, with an arrow like a sunbeam
lucid and straight, he knocks her down at his feet
O that joyful poet! O but he's sad now.

Just look at that golden neck,
those small beryl eyes, mythic, heavenly beauty —
you don't fly anymore — you don't shine,
don't sing — you're not even enough for supper.

THEY PLOW

Arano

Rust-red rows of new grape leaves
shine in the field. Morning fog
steams up from the brush,

and they plow: one shouts, prodding
slow cows, another casts seed; a third
swings his mattock slowly in ditches.

Watching from the mulberries,
the sparrow knows what's up and thrills —
the robin, too: The clever song
sparkles like gold.

THAT DAY

Quel giorno

After quarrelsome chirping
the sparrows left the Cura's
balconies among the elms.

How many times she heard the bronze
chatter of bells that day, how many swallows
fussing at noisy offspring!

Now in afternoon silence
a chair scrapes the floor, a skirt suddenly rustles —
the face of a woman — curious now —
appears at the window.

O VAIN DREAM

O vano sogno

Maybe I'm dreaming —
myrtle erupts at the edge of a hay field road —
we eat radicchio and burnet.

I lift pitchforks of sweet forage
to the wind's sound;
I visit my dear cattle.

What a sweet dream of rising with you
when cyclamen flowers in the thicket.
But rising from a summer bed
this scholar dusts his Calepine study.

The blackbird chuckles, the snipe whistles,
and I go back to singing in Latin.

Calepine — The classical scholar references his copy of
Ambroglio Calepino's 1520 Latin *Dictionarium.*

THE WIZARD

Il mago

"Roses in the garden, sparrows on the balcony!"

He speaks, and fluttering wings surround us;
the thorn bush blooms at his sweet words.
The wise one could do something else, but no:
The sky sings to, earth perfumes him.

He sends his envoys to the native dawn,
entwines their blond locks in their crowns.

In this elaborate, Symbolist allegory, as Gianfranca Lavezzi notes,
the poet-wizard dispatches his envoys, i.e., verses (those "locks" are their
words) to invite the sun to rise in the morning

UP HIGH

In alto

If my heart were strong as the wings of those swifts!

I would love this black and faithless earth
and breeze above it with sharp cries,
cavorting!
But now the sky seems to mock me
as I walk on, bent and slow.

GLORY

Gloria

— Aren't you coming up the holy mountain, Belacqua? —

Not me! — Who'll carry me up there?
Glory's far off and wears you out;
that door doesn't open for the asking.

And it's fine here in the shade of this rock,
where I listen to cicadas in sun,
and frogs croaking: *Water, water.*

Belacqua — a figure of indolence, from Dante's *Purgatorio* (IV), where
the pilgrim encounters him content to linger in the shade of a rock instead
of taking on the ardors of ascending Mount Purgatory.

CONTRAST

Contrasto

I.

I take a bit of silica and quartz:
grind, breathe, blow — and look:
the bottle's like a day in March,
blue and gray, turbid — serene!
I make the sky from a bit of sand
and my own breath. Behold: I'm an artist.

II.

I go out looking, searching, alone,
really alone, silent, head bent to earth:
Sometimes I choose one stone from thousands,
clean, grind, cut, polish, and edge —
who I am's no count: Here's a ruby;
look at the topaz; take this amethyst.

As Lavezzi notes, this meta-poem contrasts the "artist's" yearning
for fame, the "sonorous and sparkling," to the poet who aspires to
"the beautiful and good."

MIDNIGHT

Mezzanotte

for A.B.

Eight . . . nine . . . one more stroke, an hour's run by
slowly, and another . . . another. A dog whines.
An owl sobs from who-knows-what tower.

Midnight: the sound of two feet.
On distant roads, the rumbling
cart axles stop

at a blow. Everything's shut,
no form, color, life. In the center
of the sleeping city there's just
one window, one light, a pupil —

A BLACK CAT

Un gatto nero

— open. You who wake in the lamp-lit room —
what keeps you up?
that old pain, some new hope?

You search for a True One. Your thought's
an immense sea — in the immense sea,
a shell — in the shell,

a pearl: You want it. Old man, your face
is a great snowy woods in the first
slow scirocco. A black cat, with gloomy
sphynx-face, opens green eyes on you . . .

As noted in the introduction, this is a companion poem to the preceding.

AND THEN?

Dopo?

Maybe she's a good widow ... her child
comes asking for stories
while she's basting and sewing,

sits at her feet; she tells him about *The Mouse*
and *The Magician* ... at the seam,
he softly whispers, *And then?* —

— Tales all spun, there's more to sew;
the mouse dead, the magician vanished,
the boy asleep on the stool
between her knees, her needle keeps ticking.

A SOUND

Un rumore

Girl . . . your hand flies
above an acid page: you create:
your eyes look around for a word.

And the mute lamp gives you
that wincing word whereat your pen
takes to the road again, scratching away.

Shh! a sound . . . the pen goes to your lips
a foot swings . . . What is it? Nothing —
a woodworm, the door shakes — O! mamma
sleeps and dreams . . . you're married.

POOR GIFT

Povero dono

Put it down — put the gun down. Hope
one final time. Wait and keep waiting
for the cock to sing the black city away.

The cock will sing, the worms draw back.
The cursed witch standing right there
with murderous eyes will flee.

And you'll see your dead mother,
her sad face at prayer . . . she prays
you'll be content with this poor gift
she made you one day.

THE OX

Il bove

When the ox looks through vague mists
at the delicate stream, his eyes transform it:
A wide blue river winds through the steppe
to an always more distant sea.

In dawn's granular light, willow and alder
reach to heaven
a flock grazes, and it seems
the ancient god's herd.

Gargoyle wings unfurl
in the sky, chimeras soar, silent
as clouds in those heights.

A tremendous sun sinks behind
highest mountains; the huge shadows
of a measureless world turn black.

THE OLIVE TREE'S SUNDAY

La domenica dell'ulivo

Today the birds have finished their nest
(today's the olive tree festival)
with dry leaves, bits of root, twigs;

this from cypress, that from laurel.
A golden light trembles along stream banks,
through woods and shade:

And they brood on moss and lichens,
mutely fixing the crystalline sky
with sudden vibrations: a hum
of bees, flight of beetles.

STORM

Temporale

Distant tumult —

Volcanic horizon,
sea seeming aflame:
pitch dark, toward mountain,
white-streaked clouds:
in blackness
a hut

a gull's
wing.

AFTER THE DOWNPOUR

Dopo l'acquazzone

Pelting and hissing, the black nimbus passed.
Now the church bell rings; the red roof gleams;
the fresh smell of boxwood
    drifts from the churchyard.

Near the church, while the bell
tingles, sings, and tolls;
a shouting gang plays hide-and-seek
    at the stone cross.

Rain veils the horizon;
but the fragrance lingers
under calm sky; a rainbow bends
    from mountain to mountain.

OCTOBER EVENING

Sera d'ottobre

Along the street, vermilion berries
laugh in clusters on the bushes.
From plowed fields, cows return
      late to their crib.

A poor man comes down the street
dragging his way through loud leaves.
In the fields, a girl sings to the wind,
      O thorn flowers! . . .

THE LAST SONG

L'ultimo canto

Only that field where I slowly turn
remains yellow with maize,
turning the pale sun paler.

A delicate wind stirs the husks;
a storm of sparrows flies off
into a sky of washed violet.

A woman harvester sings at full voice:
Love begins with music and song
and ends with tears in the heart.

BENEDICTION

Benedizione

It's evening: The patient
priest walks very slowly,
raised hand blessing
what he sees and hears.

He reverently blesses:
all of it: all the good village,
even the ryegrass there in the grain,
even the snake here in the flowers.

Every branch, every bird,
yes, of woods and house roof
he has blessed in passing;

also the hawk, also the little
black hawk in the violet sky,
even the crow, and the poor little man

up there in the graveyard,
digging and digging all day.

WITH THE ANGELS

Con gli angioli

The lilacs and the wood laurel were in flower;
she sewed the wedding dress:

The sky hadn't opened its starry bowls;
the sensitive plant hadn't closed

But when she laughed; laughed, O sudden
black swifts: But with whom? At what?

She laughed with the angels, with those
golden clouds, those rose-color clouds.

One of Pascoli's letters, Lavezzi notes, records a Romagnolo
("perhaps also Tuscan") adage, that when one laughs
spontaneously to oneself, one "laughs with the angels."

THE BEGGAR

Il mendico

A tramp's dining between
two fountains in the ruins;
eyes looking west
he eats bread from both hands.

A charm runs through his head:
This hand holds meat, and this one bread.
Amid croaking frogs
a wise magus feasts.

He rises, drinks from two fountains:
clear water from this one,
sweet wine from that.

He lies down; looks up
at moonlit mountains;
he works his arts on the violet dark —

                                   a canopy

of miraculous work,
pierced with stars of gold.

THE SEA

Il mare

I put my face to the window and watch the sea:
Stars pass, waves rise and fall.
I see the stars pass; I see the waves pass:
A fish breaks, the heart skips a beat.

Here water sighs, wind alights,
a silver bridge appears on the sea.

O bridge thrown across serene lakes
for whom are you made and where do you lead?

THE LITTLE PLOWMAN

Il piccolo aratore

He writes . . . (grandma admires):
such beautiful plowing.
He guides the plow slowly by hand,
hoes, and sows his field:
the field is white; the seeds are black.

He plows in winter: The black winter seed
springs up, leafs-out to flower in spring;

and now the first sounds of March
spin in the sky, and the snake leaves its hole.

DREAM

Sogno

For the length of a breath I was back
in my village, my house. Nothing had changed.
Tired, come back as if from a voyage: Tired,
to my father, to the dead, I'd returned.

I felt great joy, great pain, sweetness,
and mute disquiet — Mamma?
There she is: Cooking a bit of supper for you.
Poor Mamma! — And I didn't see her.

THE NEST

Il nido

A nest hangs from the skeletal
wild rosebush, where in spring
a loud chirping of nestlings
bursts from the river.

Now there's only one feather,
fluttering, hesitant, in a breath of wind,
that ancient dream of a harsh soul,
fleeing forever and never gone.

And the eye already turns from the sky,
from the sky where a final chorus rose,
radiated, and vanished,

to fix on earth
where leaves rot, and waves of wind
break in a lonely country.

LIGHTNING

Lampo

And *what was* made heaven and earth:

The breathless earth suddenly livid.
Occluded sky, tragic, undone:
White white in silent tumult.
A house flashed, gone in an instant,
like a wide-open, terrified
eye shut in black night.

THUNDER

Il tuono

And there was night and void:

Suddenly a cliff
gave way, split open
boomed, rebounded, rolled
over its own dark sound,
fell silent, and farther off resounded,
and was gone. And then he heard
mother singing softly,
and the cradle rocking.

THE BLIND

I ciechi

Dog days, they sit along the ditch
beyond the storm of village churchbells.
Trotting horses raise the dust —
hoofbeats, a quarrel, old song:

and then the grave psalm of earth,
a prayer to that presence.
— *Our daily bread* — they cry away—
our daily ... our ... you, Jesus, you said so.

SNOWY NIGHT

Notte di neve

The bell shouts, *Peace!*
but far off, faintly. There,

where the shadow falls silent
a marble graveyard rises;
its glow, wide and fleeting
dissolves into black sky.
Peace! Peace! Peace! Peace!
And darkness is white.

SNOWFALL

Nevicata

It snows: The air's a confusion of whiteness
on white earth; snow upon snow:
Elms moan, tall and tired — masses
of whiteness fall with soft thuds.

The snow blows; winds crash;
The storm whirls down the streets.
Children pass, and they're crying.
A mother goes by in prayer.

SORROWFUL NIGHT

Notte dolorosa

The sky goes its way, quiet and distant:

Earth sleeps — the sky lets it sleep.
The waters sleep, mountains, moors ...
— But no: He hears the sea's breath,
moaning, he hears the dark huts.
There's a child inside who can't sleep:
He cries, and the stars slowly pass.

SIREN

La sirena

Evenings, in the slow whisper
of waves nursing the sands,
a lament rises from the foggy sea—
your song, O Siren.

And it seems to rise, to rise
then break with a heavy moan.
The wave sighs among weeds
and a ghost ship passes:

The vanishing shadow of a ship
in gray mist; and the fading cry
of those hearts
that turn to shore —

the fleeting shore, already
slipping into haze, gone,
bearing off all, the churches
intoning their Hail Marys,

houses on the cliff
barely glowing through that gray,
and the shadow of smoke rising
perhaps after supper.

THE HEART OF THE CYPRESS

Il cuore del cipresso

I.
O cypress, alone and black you break
the glassy sky above scrubland
bristling with thistle, shrill with whipsnakes.

Often, in blackberry season,
children hear a secret whisper in you,
a nest dreaming in your heart.

The last hatching. You sing softly,
hermit cypress, while your shadow
lengthens in the graveyard,
as if looking for an urn with those limbs.

II.
Shorter days, and the shadow, short-lived,
lingers and searches, unquiet, for sun;
and the sun is cold, the cloudless sky pale.

Early evening: shadow enters that shadow
where stars wander alone.
Brambles redden, thorns choke

every path through the wine-color leaf fall.
(You sway with indifference, hermit cypress.)
The first rains whistle,
and gray winds wail and toll.

III.
And your nest? Your nest? ... The wind
wails, batters, endlessly beats you.
You rise and remain, like Death.

And your heart? Your heart ... rain
thrashes the window where I see you:
a black fog in gray fog.

And your dream? Behold earth vanish:
Snow falls, mute in the guise of thought.
You stand in this white, silent snowslide,
gigantic, unmoveably black.

CHESTNUT TREE

Il castagno

For Francesco Pellegrini

I.

When the apple flowered and leafed out again
and the quince tree flowered
the blue slope seemed

          a dream sky.

You were bare; and the violets
had already been gathered from every shore.
You let all your sun fall through

          onto grasses and brush.

And, sacred chestnut, with branches
barely recovered from mists and sleet,
you covered yourself bit by bit

          with light green foam.

But then, when you saw mountain girls
under heavy burdens wipe their faces,
(you knew them when snows made them

          come down the mountain) —

you felt for them,
and wove a cool shadow above the torrent
at the ravine's edge, stirring

          with reed warbler song.

II.
And you already hid something
in the sharp, shut burr, as a good grandfather
hides a late, simple gift in his hand
                              covered with hair.

At the first cold, when the good rustic
numbered his children again at the fire
and with him the mountain wind slowly,
                              hoarsely grumbled;

you scattered those spiny nuts
on yellowed heather in the storms
and opened them out of pity
                              for those poor fingers ...

scattered all the spiny balls and delicate fronds,
and everyone took them, that festive poor crowd.
You stood naked then, your branches
                              despoiled, O huge one,

and saw the vines and the apple tree
clothed in gold and purple already reflected
in snow, and the black cypress
                              in a dull sky.

III.
Thanks to you, huts warm to the cauldron's
golden churning as it sways on its chain.
Thanks to you, the flame crackles and shines
                              under that bubbling;

you, pious chestnut, you alone, give such gifts
to the peasant who has nothing but sun,
you alone give that berry, the greatest good,
                              to his offspring;

the brown heifer has a warm bed
thanks to you and doesn't need hay,
and limping grandfather has your beautiful,
                              crackling flame,

whose sharp joy bursts the bark
on your branches. The grateful pot
seethes with your fruit. The wind sweeps
                              your branch to the window.

It snows on the white mountains.
It still snows. Grandfather's happy; he repeats
the ancient proverb: *The more snow*
                    the more chestnuts.

THE LILIES

I gigli

In my village, behind the *Madonna*
of the Waters, near a thousand pious whispers
my lilies rise

                    on slender green columns:

Mine; for my sad mother planted
these bulbs in a corner of her garden.
It's gone to others now: nothing's left (there was so much! ...)
                  of my mother's.

So many years! ... But yearly the lilies still rise
to whiten thick nettle baskets;
and now ... now maybe they've been
                  already gathered.

Maybe they've been placed on the altar
already, in a prayer for rain,
or for the wheat harvest, or the maize;
                  and in quiet afternoon prayer,

gazing at those lilies, some woman
fleetingly remembers — asks that Mary
take me home to die in peace,
                  close to my dead.

FINAL DREAM

Ultimo sogno

In the rigid crash of iron
carriages hurtling toward the infinite,
among sudden bumps and savage jolts ...
a sudden silence. I was healed.

The cloud of my illness dissolved
in a breath. Eyelids trembling,
I saw my mother at my bedside:
I watched without marvel.

Free! ... yes, numb, perhaps if I wanted
to free the hands at my chest —
but I didn't want to. One heard a subtle
rustling, persistent, as of cypresses;

as of a river searching for the nonexistent sea
across an immense plain:
I followed this vain whispering
always the same, always more distant.

from **SONGS OF CASTELVECCHIO**

Canti di Castelvecchio (1898–1902)

FOG

Nebbia

Hide the distant things,
you, untouchable, colorless fog,
you, smoke that still roils
            at dawn
from streetlamps and the dizzy
            plummeting landslides!

Hide the distant things,
hide the dead from me!
that I might see only
            the garden hedge,
the wall with valerian rooted
            in every crack.

Hide the distant things:
things drunk with tears!
That I might only see two apples,
            two peaches,
that give their sweet honey
            for my black bread.

Hide the distant things
that want me to love and go!
that I might only see
            the street's whiteness

and have something to do at the tired
        don don of bells ...

Hide the distant things,
hide them, wrap them
in the heart's flight, that I might only
        see the cypress, there, alone,
here, only this garden,

        my dog dozing close by.

TWO WANDERERS

I due girovaghi

We're alone. The white sky
turns like a windmill.
Two of us on the solitary earth,
two of us walking, always.
Just my rags, just yours
on this road. No sound
but our two cries:

> — *I'm here today*
> *and tomorrow I'm gone.*
> — *Winnowing-sieves!*
> *Winnowing-sieves! Sieves!*

Me, here, knocking my teeth,
you, there, pounding your feet;
I don't see you, but you hear me.
I hear you, but you don't see me.
We hurl our cries
like abandoned dogs
at the doorways:

> — *I'm here today*
> *and tomorrow I'm gone.*
> — *Winnowing-sieves!*
> *Winnowing-sieves! Sieves!*

This world has certain doors
where you enter and never leave.
It's the castle of death.
You hear the grass grow,
the grass and the poppies,
here, at night, in good times:
but nothing else . . .

> — *I'm here today*
> *and tomorrow I'm gone.*
> — *Winnowing-sieves!*
> *Winnowing-sieves! Sieves!*

We meet up . . . Do I mock you?!
No, bosom friend, you're my brother!
It's a pointless shouting in frigid wind.
And no face appears, saying
Oh, just a chimneysweep . . .
just to say, Oh, just a little old man . . .
some chaff in the grain . . .

> *Sieves!*
> *Winnowing-sieves! Sieves!*

BAGPIPES

Le ciaramelle

I heard the bagpipes in my sleep
I heard the sound of lullabies.
All the stars are in the sky.
All the lamps in the huts.

Wordlessly the pipers come
come down to the huts
from dark mountains
to awaken all the godly poor.

Everyone's out of bed;
hanging from its beam, the lamp has been lit.
They know that yawning half-light,
careful steps, lowered voices ...

The pious lamps burn all around
there in the house, here in the bushes.
The vast earth's
a little diorama at daybreak.

All the stars stand waiting
in dawn's first blue, and now
the sweet sound of church
comes from the bagpipes.

The sound of cloister,
of home and cradle,
of mamma, all our sweet,
lost weeping for nothing.

O bagpipes of those first years,
before the day, before the true,
as the stars fade, conscious
of our brief mystery —

who haven't started the bread
who haven't lit the fire —
you make us cry a bit
before the bells ring.

Not for nothing now, but for something,
for many things! But the heart wants
that great sobbing that comes to a rest,
that great pain that stops hurting:

It wants the true pain more than the new,
sobbing beyond reason,
on its martyrdom, on its pleasure,
it wants those good ancient tears.

THE TABLECLOTH

La tovaglia

They call you: — Girl!
so you're never still,
evening to morning,
but put it where you took it,
the white tablecloth
just after supper! Watch out
lest the dead come,
the sad, the pale dead!

They enter, mute, panting.
Everyone's so tired!
They stay, seated all night
around that whiteness.
There till morning,
hats held between hands,
without feeling a thing
under a lamp that's gone out. —

The girl's already grown;
she runs the house and she works:
does the wash and cooks,
does it, all just as then.
Thinks of everything
but clearing the table.
She lets the dead come,
the good, the poor dead.

135

O, the black, black night
of wind, water, snow.
She lets them in at evening,
with their gentle longing
around the table,
resting till daybreak,
looking for distant things,
hats held between hands.

From evening till morning
searching for distant things
they stay, faces bent
over some crumbs of bread,
drinking bitter tears
wanting to remember.
O, the dead don't remember,
her dear, dear dead!

— Bread, yes . . . it's called bread,
that we break together,
remember? . . . and checkered linen,
there was a lot: remember? . . .
These? . . . Here are two,
like yours and you,
our two bitter tears
fallen in memory! —

LITTLE BEGGAR

Fanciullino mendico

My heart bears the sad words
    of that child who comes to my door —
I shed a tear, just one,
    for poverty's hurt.

Though I thought it fell unfelt
    in that mop of curls,
he raised those piercing eyes,

And as if I were asking forgiveness
    I stilled the lost tear with a kiss,
and put my offering
    in his poor fingers.

And then I felt in my heart
    the voice now as then:
I don't want it: Sir, I don't want
    to cheapen your pity.

And when he was past the gate
    and back on his lonely path
I felt he liked bearing
    that heavy pack,

and called his mother, who seemed
        to rise from distant clouds,
and watch him. So they were: she
        dead, dead! And him without bread.

THE VINE

La vite

Now that the cuckoo is near
and the peach tree in flower,
> I go out — the pruning hook
> hangs in its place for me.

I carry my blade, for I already hear
the cuckoo's first sound:
> *cu . . . cu . . .* and I answer in kind:
> He tells me, *cu cu,* and yes, I *cut.*

Yes, I cut you, vine, for I already hear
bees shrill in sun.
> I cut all the old growth.
> I leave you three eyes and two heads.

O, are you crying, gentle vine,
because you're naked, newborn in wind?
> If only I too were a pruned vine
> among the flowers of April!

Do you cry over what's lost?
But I cut, trim and carry away
> so you'll have your great clusters
> at leaf fall.

O my vine . . . — no: my vitals
twisted so, bursting into greater fruit!
        And after . . . how good the smell
        of poplar buds on the fingers!

And to speak right to them,
with that bird come across the sea,
        asking in the midst of my work
        how many years I'll live.

THE NAP

Il sonnellino

I watched, in sleep's shadow
already black, something lost
in there: The sky held nothing
      but a rose-color cirrus.

And that cirrus in the limpid blue
shined on gray castles
raising a whisper
      of birds

singing above
red roof-tiles and rivers.
And then there was nothing
      but silence, oblivion.

They sang as if they only knew
to sing the heart's dreams,
strong
      and soundless.

And I returned to sleep's caress
a pink sleep, searching
searching, searching for
      that old *something*;

and perhaps I saw and took it,
guided by a bird song
from who-knows-what unknown,
        more beautiful countries ...

I scarely saw — and I turned —
so beautiful, better to see them, the best ones ...
But a thunderclap snatched it all away,
        O, sudden thunder!

Changing a pleasant
sleepy dawn, elided in sleep
into a shrill and
        drawn-out day!

THE BICYCLE

La bicicletta

I.
I seemed to hear a nestling
stir in the hedge.
A moment ... I took in the river's
        dark rumbling.

I seemed to make out a sea
gilded with trembling grain.
A heartbeat ... I saw a row
        of black cypresses.

I seemed to slice through the cry
of a sorrowful, long cortege.
A palpitation ... Nuptials and love
        passed close.

                dlin ... dlin ...

II.
The shouts of the nameless
crowd still echoed;
I heard locusts screech
        on humid earth.

Someone who plowed the fields
said his brief words to me:
You — keep your scythe in hand
when you rest.

I spoke a wingèd word to you,
flighty virgin;
Talking to herself,
an old woman heard it.

dlin . . . dlin . . .

III.
My earth, fleeting road
do you run on or do I?
No matter. Whether I come, or you go
it's the same farewell.

But beautiful: this feeling of wings
and gratitude for the thrill of day.
Rest is so sweet . . . and night
already falls: I return.

The little lamp burns
through the dark city,
and the little bell rings more slowly:
a little push, and it goes . . .

dlin . . . dlin . . .

NOCTURNAL JASMINE

Il gelsomino notturno

And the night-flowers open
at the hour I think of my dear ones;
        sunset's butterflies
        hover in the viburnum.

After a bit the bird song ceases.
and there's just a whispering house.
        Nests fall asleep below wings
        like eyes below closed lids.

The strawberries' fragrance
pours from calices,
        and a lamp glows in a room over there.
        Grass sprouts above ditches.

A late bee whispers,
finding the cells already closed.
        Pleiades course the blue,
        stars all twinkling.

All night one breathes
night's windy perfume.
        A lamp climbs the stairs,
        illumines the second floor and goes dark.

Then dawn: Crumpled a bit,
the petals close, and I don't know
what new joy comes
to life in a soft, secret urn.

in un angolo

gra a un miglio

che limpido e

dell'ore

all'ombre

verde,

spughe bru

...n molti secoli o un anno
e quelle nubi se vanno.
immoto qui.
È dolce qui rimanere
lo moto d'ali e di fronde,
il gallo che da un podere
e da un altro l'altro risponde;
e altrove l'uomo è passa,
d'una uscia che russa.

nuovi suoni, ed aggiungi
accento di meraviglia.
                    e più
ncora l'ora, che manda
suo grido di meraviglia,
e quindi con le sue blande
rima prega e consiglia
                m'incuora

IV. APPENDIX:
A POET OF DEAD LANGUAGE

Un poeta di lingua morta

This sea is full of voices, and this sky is full of visions. Forgotten Nereids lament in this sea, and often the dead cities flutter, suspended from this sky.

This is a sacred place, where the Greek waves come in search of the Latin, and here they break, forming in the morning's serenity an immense scintillating bath in the liquefaction, and here they slow down leaving, among the vapors of evening, images of great iridescent purple, of seashells' every color. A sacred place. Between Scilla and Messina,[1] they say, death lurks in the sea's depths, below the bluest cobalt, below the scintillating metals of dawn and iridescent purple dusk; death lurks, not death that gathers — now flower and now fruit — from the human plants, leaving the branches free to flower and fruit again, but death which dessicates the plants themselves; not that which prunes, but that which uproots, not that which leaves behind tears, but that which is followed by oblivion. Such power, hidden where ruins and rubble radiate, has annulled such history here, beauty, and greatness. That which remains is only a track in the sky, an echo of the sea. Here, where history has been all but destroyed, poetry remains.

And the poet was in this country where I've only been a few days.[2] Who told me about him when I was still a young man—oh my! more than thirty

---

1. [Translator] The straits of Messina, known to English speakers as Scylla and Charybdis.

2. [Translator] The subject of Pascoli's essay, Diego Vitrioli (1818–1898), was a classicist renowned for his original poetry in Latin.

years ago—at college in Urbino? An old friar who also knew the gifts of the muses, Father Giacoletti, whose name, so far as I know, doesn't extend beyond the melancholy cloister of the seminary.[3] He was much esteemed for Latin poems on optics—of all things—and on the steam locomotive.

This old friar, for whom we had an almost fearful admiration, often spoke of a poet, a Latinist, who lived far away, in the extreme reaches of Italy, compared to whom he was nothing,

I still haven't forgotten those supreme words of praise and that approbation (the good friar chopped the air like Galdino Manzoniano when he spoke),[4] that nod to the infinite distance.

Thus when I found myself on that edge of Italy for a few days, I suddenly thought again of that poet, the Genius of the Place. He was indeed a poet, and the poet, you know, is virtually a creator, since it is he who with words— *fiat lux*—suddenly illuminates the surrounding darkness. Certainly star and flower, serenity and storm existed before the poet spoke of them and you had eyes to see them; but you didn't look, and beautiful things were as if they didn't exist: It was his word that created them for you. And thus I thought of this poet at the far reaches of Italy, where Greek waves merge with Latin, as a mysteriously remote spirit that woke from his cave to create this fantastic world with Nereids crying from the sea and dead cities suspended in the sky. He had the air, this poet who lived apart from the world, if I'm permitted to say it, of a Proteus, old sea dog, who knew all the whirlpools of the sea.

---

3. [Translator] As Pascoli notes, Giuseppe Giacoletti (1803–1865) was a teacher and Latin poet. His poem on the steam locomotive (*De lebetis materie et forma eiusque tutela in machinis vaporis vi agentibus*) won the prestigious international *Certamen poeticum Hoeufftianum* for Latin poetry, awarded in Holland, of which Vitrioli was the first recipient. (See note 8, below.)

4. [Translator] A character from Manzoni's *I promessi sposi (The Betrothed)*.

I

And he was old and solitary, and steered clear of commerce and the sight of men. They say that he only frequented solitary places when he went out walking: and for what if not for to listen to what the creatures of his poems whispered? To return to his own world ripped from our impassable ocean of death? Because he was truly an ancient, an escapee to the past, a survivor in the ruins of pagan poetry, and he felt that agony of the past and showed to the light-hearted or indifferent of our time—ours and not his—a face that seemed to cringe with contempt but was really in pain. Smiling, he said he had lived alongside Cicero and Virgil, and it pleased him to live so now. But I will go farther. The Greek was in him, and some of his poems felt the ardent softness of his most ancient fellow citizen, Ibico.[5] It's hardly worth adding that he also made poems in Greek with elegant ease. But, Greek or Latin, he scorned the present, not only in literature and philology, but a bit in everything. In sum, he lived among vanished things, and his thought constantly needed to resuscitate dead beauties.

He was, if you will, the last of the humanists, and beyond the cult of poetry and ancient literature had something else in common with, if not with many, at least some them: the reconciliation in his own heart—if not formally—of paganism and Christian devotion. For a moment I remember that Poliziano and Pico della Mirandola wanted to be buried in Dominican tunics,[6] and perhaps because he also had it inscribed in Latin on his coffin, everyone knows that he was most pious and said multiple—I think five—rosaries a

---

5. [Translator] 6th century BCE Greek poet of Reggio, trained in the school of Stesichorus.

6. [Translator] Poliziano (1454–1494), the Florentine classicist and translator of Homer and Catullus among others, was a poet in his own right, his "Manto" much praised for its homage to Virgil. Pico della Mirandola (1463–1494), the famed Neoplatonist philosopher and humanist, famously the author of the *Oration on the Dignity of Man*. Poliziano and Pico were buried together and were possibly lovers. Their deaths have been attributed to arsenic poisoning, perhaps at the hands of a Medici.

day. Noteworthy, too, is the friendship that he shared with the old pontiff; a friendship in which religious sensibility mattered at least as much as the sharing of study and pleasure.[7]

Two old ones: This great priest, very old, careworn, almost diaphanous, who rules the conscience of so many million, who stands an inflexible guard of the past and hints at raiding the future world, and who, in the nocturnal silence of the Vatican, chisels a humble prayer to Mary and the precepts of sobriety for attaining a long life—and this other old man who wandered along the Ionian meditating upon the elegy of roses and two embracing skeletons in Pompeii! These two old ones intended and offered their graceful *Carmina* to each other in elegant editions and exchanged honest praise. They traded gold for gold, not as sometimes happens, when each throws back a reflection of the other's little coin from a vast heap of small change.

And if not unique, it was nevertheless fine gold, fine gold work from one of them. No labor of these patient artificers of Latinity had ever been so celebrated as this poem, perhaps the first of the poet from Reggio, the *Xiphias*, which was prized half a century ago by the Dutch Royal Academy (then called the Belgian Institute).[8] And as a boy I heard that that poem was the best branch to flower—as Regaldi puts it[9]—from that dead tree of classical antiquity. Time hasn't altered that judgment.

Thus, for a few months now, watching that sea and shore that were so limpidly described in the poem, I thought with veneration, yes, of the old wizard who knew how to create such a living thing from a dead language.

---

7. [Translator] The pontiff is Leo XIII, with whom Vitrioli had a warm friendship.

8. [Translator] In 1845, Vitrioli's poem "Xiphias" won the first gold medal awarded in the *Certamen poeticum Hoeufftianum* international contest in Latin poetry, in Amsterdam. The work is a mythological treatment of the swordfish living in the straits of Scylla and Charybdis. Vitrioli was so proud of his award that he is said to have dined on swordfish on the anniversary of his triumph.

9. [Translator] Giuseppe Regaldi (1809–1883) founded a school devoted to improvisational poetry.

II

And I'd wanted to see him. It seemed to me that only by seeing and speaking with him would I have the whole of the vision that enchanted me.

I heard the poetry. I wanted to see the poet. I landed on the shore of Ibico with a ship that resembled a trireme. I landed one beautiful morning and went hesitantly, a Tyrrhenian guest, to the Greek poet, at the height of his years and glory.

And had the old poet encouraged me, I would have said:

Poet, why do you write in a language that no longer sounds on the lips of the living? Why do you only want poets to understand you? If you're looking for the praises of the many, why do you turn to the few? If you aim to be useful to many, inspiring, as you say, modesty, valor, sense, compassion, honest will in the human breast, why privilege only some to your harmonious admonitions? Why this solitude? Why this separateness that seems to reprove others? Ibico, your ancient fellow citizen, went city to city, island to island, and country to country: You close the doors, so that the sound of your lyre doesn't reach the ear of the passerby. Poet, open the Muse's house. Let your sweet hymns be understood by all: Sing them in our language and present, so that all of us can understand them. We have such need of that! For our soul is deformed by the hold of reality and needs beauty. It grows sad at the spectacle of unwarranted suffering and of undeserved happiness—the soul needs justice. The soul is consumed with envy, it melts with compassion, and has need of purification. And you can reveal beauty and can rouse justice, and you can complete our catharsis, O poet, you can do this, all this, and don't you want to? Poet, take a step, just one step down to us, and we, softened, ravished, will climb a slope of infinite grades to win our small share of your sublimity.

Thus I would have spoken to the old poet; but I didn't, because he had died, the news thereof reawakening at once his slumbering fame, like the breath of breeze a smoldering fire. And I will not look for my words to be answered, because, as his Ibico said, one can no longer find the elixir of life for those who have died!

Still I dare, though I don't fancy my small mind has much in common with his great one, I dare imagine his response.

III

He might have answered me: My guest, I will speak to you with ancient simplicity. You don't have doubts about my art because the language which is its instrument isn't universally understood. You know very well that I couldn't use a language understood by all, because such a language doesn't still exist. And I'm not just saying that there isn't such a common language, but such a language intelligible to all—even by the greater part of one people—can't exist. Nor can we hope that such a language, whether universal or national, can arise, or fear that one can be manufactured by our mechanics: Nature goes from the simple to the composite, from the homogeneous to the heterogeneous and not vice-versa, and languages and dialects will always multiply, year by year and century by century. For this reason, my guest, I use Latin and Greek as I would any spoken language; indeed, if you consider it well, I have to believe I have more connoisseurs of my Latin works in the world than I do of my Italian writings in all of Italy. But this isn't the source of your doubt. Finally, you're not talking about language—the sensible garment—but the idea, that is, the intelligible soul. You note that even in Italian, I prefer the antiquated word and superannuated construction. You consider the sixteenth-century taste of my *Pompeian Vigils* and all my vernacular work, my worship of the Latin language and the Greek in *Xiphias*, in the elegies, epigrams, inscriptions, epistles, orations: the greater part of my work, and you say that I repudiate the present for the past and don't want to be of my time. Oh! Be careful. My idea is this. A person continuously staves off death. He must contend with death, oppose, extract what he can. Ours is a cold life and we need warmth; our life is dark and we need light; one who can give warmth and light, and doesn't let it go out: A spark can reawaken the flame, and joy! One won't let death touch what was beautiful or happy. And we console the banqueters who have so much wine on the table at first that it seems excessive, if they grow sad at the end because their thirst is unsatisfied:

155

We console them with the cheap amphora that we had put away while they were smiling. And if this our fame doesn't reach far and wide and our voice doesn't leave the shadows of classrooms, be patient! I feel that poetry and religion are one thing, and that as religion requires concentration and mystery and silence and words that veil and therefore conceal their meaning—I mean words foreign to common usage, so poetry also in the vernacular needs what has never been found in the language, forms, or habitual rhythms. I do not believe that poetry must or can be the agitator of disorder, but rather the Beatrice of hearts. She doesn't blow out her cheeks to play the trumpet, but briefly draws her fingers across the harp. Poetry doesn't repel, filling itself with din and manic ears and brains, but draws others to herself with a faint and distant ringing. There are certain kinds of music that need to be heard from the distance if one is to enjoy them without being overwhelmed. In the case of poetry, one has to draw close in order to hear it. And it speaks now to this one and now to that, dries a tear here, drawing a sigh there, with delicate modesty, like a silent benefactress. Now the people whom my ancient lyre attracts with its happy sound, and consoles and comforts, come from all parts of the world and will come till one studies the language of the Choirs. Oh! The great future of this universal art!

IV

I think he would have answered me thus, plumbing the equanimity of his placid old age for his poetry's rationale. But I didn't fathom his voice and won't hear it again. I have reread his written soul in order to reconstruct it in myself. I've reread his Pompeian elegies, vibrant with passion, his Greek and Latin epigrams with their bitter smile, his inscriptions of noble Romanitas, his prose—to tell the truth, too flowery, the Asino Pontaniano,[10] too sharp—to speak honestly—in its pedantic comedy, the Xiphias ... remains his best work, and it would displease him to hear it said, but it is so. Rich with all the sweetness of spring, the first flower the plant brought forth was—as often happens—the most beautiful. Later, it was his sea that inspired him and childhood observations that nourished that inspiration.

In his first work, he is a realist, so to speak, but he projected the truth he saw and best rendered, he luminously projected onto the mythic past. Caritone is a young fisherman, of our times and our sea, who knows all the fish and their relative value; Umbrone is an old sea dog like many, everywhere along these coasts, and Clite is the beautiful, ardent, demanding Calabrian girl we know so well; but in those far-off depths, illuminated by the poet's art, they seem grander and more beautiful.

It is the work of a modern hand, interred—in a certain way—in the patina and cast of antiquity, but the hand is of a Michelangelo or, better, a Cellini. The illusion is grand and compels us to say that few Alexandrian and Roman poets would have known how to make a poem so perfect, moving with equally native grace between modern and ancient styles, between the memories of Homer's world and Hesiod's, and the everyday particulars of house and street.[11]

---

10. [Translator] *The Pontinian Ass — A Dialogue between two Jokers* published in 1892. The title page tells us that the book was dictated in Latin and translated into "volgare favella" or Italian by the author.

11. [Translator] The phrase "between the style of the moderns and the ancient tongue" is taken from sonnet 7 of Petrarch's *Rime*.

Oh! Could I have heard such a thing from your mouth, oh poet! They say you were a full-voiced and compelling reader of your poems. I would have wanted to hear you repeat these subtlest verses that perpetuate Virgil, facing the sea that you have populated with nymphs, the boats of the swordfish fishermen, whose fables you have told the world. But now you won't recite deeply and quietly anymore—death has closed the ancient poet's mouth. Still you're not dead. Poets don't die when they leave such a life of images.

These images are his exchange for the sacred gift. They came to life for him, having been confused in darkness and chaos, so to say, of nature and the psyche, and he drew them forth and breathed them out above, and they appeared to all: Now they are the unending sound of his second life. And whoever will listen to this most beautiful sea, the voices of the triumphant fishermen resounding from the mountains, whoever fixes their eyes on an immobile fishing boat searching the depths, whoever comes to hear the cadenced ringing of cymbals, will think of you, as if alive, as if immortal, O buried poet, and seeing the fata morgana[12] rise from your grotto of iridescent shells and thicken with the sharp shuttle of wind on the warp of the dead, calm on your colorful grave, and unroll the marvelous canvas on which the city rocks and things multiply, he will repeat your name like that of a Magus, without equal and no other, oh Diego Vitrioli.

12. [Translator] A peculiar kind of mirage, but it should be noted here that La Fata Morgana is the Italian name of Morgan Le Fay, sorceress of the Arthurian legends, thus here perhaps Pascoli's reference to Vitrioli as a Magus or wizard.

lavoro per la su...

istero, ~~xxxxxx~~ anno

di Giov:

molto be

V. ACKNOWLEDGMENTS

I am profoundly grateful to my editor Nina Kamberos, without whose inestimable help and encouragement over several years this work would not have appeared. Maria Truglio's comments on the manuscript were an indispensable, life-saving guide through Pascoli's many difficulties. One could not dream of people more helpful than those of Laertes Press, and I am especially grateful to Maxine Mills for her exquisite book design, Valerie Price for her careful proof reading, Margaretta Yarborough for her review of the manuscript, and Dodd Brown for his help with the notes. With so much help, any flaws that remain are entirely my own. I also thank Biba Kayewich whose portrait of Pascoli adorns the cover. My debt of gratitude to teachers and mentors from decades ago, Franco Fido, Elizabeth Kirk, Suzanne Woods, A. S. Wensinger, Rosmarie and Keith Waldrop, and the late James Boulger and Barbara Lewalski only deepens with time. Cid Corman, Edwin Honig, and Jerome Rothenberg kept me true. My children Rebekah and Eva shined and shine the light.

di solitaria

da casa mia;

cade dall'aria

onde ove i sento

ir del grano

Giovanni Pascoli "addresses the deepest part of himself" and in doing so addresses the nature of language. Here is a moral harmony; a manifesto for a poetry of common memory and dream. Pascoli, quite simply, names truth; while of the nineteenth century, he is utterly contemporary. There is much of timeless poetics here, something of Blake's visionary innocence, something of Whitman's self-contradictions, yet Pascoli has his own tragic sadness to reconcile: He is unique.

In John Martone he has met his perfect translator. Martone matches Pascoli's erudition and intelligent ordering. He brings us a clarity from the limpid and sometimes conflicting apparent simplicity of Pascoli's work. *O Little One* is vital to everyone who loves poetry. — *Gerry Loose*

Martone's translations convey with grace the simplistic beauty of Pascoli's verse, in both prose and poetry, and allow English-speaking readers to enter into his world. Most anyone with an interest in poetry and world literature would enjoy Martone's translations, but I particularly recommend them to Italian American readers as a means of opening a window onto their cultural heritage. Pascoli's works were written during the same historical period in which the great wave of Italian emigration to America began, and they give voice to the anguish and tensions of the times. The theme of home and family as symbolic places of refuge, scenes from Italian country life and its natural surroundings, reflections on death and grief, an exploration of the relationship between language — in dialectic, standard or classical form — and transcendent understanding, and, at the heart of *O Little One*, the reliance on the spirit of one's childish self for inspiration and succor in troubling times, imbue the works that Martone has translated, and by engaging with them we can gain greater insight into the cultural elements that continue to inform contemporary Italian American identity. — *Carla Simonini*